# Contents

This volume has been compiled from texts selected from the following works by Brother Roger: *The Dynamic Of The Provisional, Festival Without End, Struggle And Contemplation, A Life We Never Dared Hope For, The Wonder Of A Love, And Your Deserts Shall Flower, A Heart That Trusts* and *Mary Mother Of Reconciliations*, as well as from articles which have appeared in *The Letter From Taizé*.

Extracts from the journals are indicated in italics.

*Brother Roger of Taizé*

# HIS LOVE IS A FIRE

CENTRAL WRITINGS
WITH
EXTRACTS FROM
JOURNALS

**GEOFFREY
CHAPMAN
MOWBRAY**

**Geoffrey Chapman Mowbray**
A Cassell imprint
Villiers House, 41–47 Strand, London WC2N 5JE

This compilation originally published as *Son amour est un feu*,
© Ateliers et Presses de Taizé 1988
Translation © Ateliers et Presses de Taizé 1990

English-language edition first published 1990
Reprinted 1990

**British Library Cataloguing in Publication Data**
Roger, *of Taizé, Brother*
  His love is a fire.
  1. France. Taizé. Men's religious communities: Communauté
  de Taizé
  I. Title   II. Son amour est un feu. *English*
  267′.23′094443

ISBN 0-264-67210-0

Typeset by Colset Pte. Ltd, Singapore
Printed and bound in Great Britain by
Biddles Ltd, Guildford and King's Lynn

*When the night becomes dark,*
*his love is a fire.*
*So fix your gaze on the lamp*
*burning in the darkness,*
*until the dawn comes*
*and the morning star rises in your hearts.*

# THE ESSENTIAL
# IS HIDDEN FROM
# OUR EYES

# Loved With Eternity's Love

'DO YOU LOVE ME?' This is the ultimate question that Jesus asks Peter. Peter, saddened and dismayed because he had denied Jesus three times over before his torture on the cross. And now the Risen Lord is standing before him. But Jesus does not condemn him for his denial. He does not adopt the attitude of someone who is stronger. He does nothing to tighten the noose of bad conscience that is already around Peter's neck. Compassion is the very heart of Christ's humanity. During his earthly life, he too has passed through ways of darkness.

Christ says only these four words to Peter. 'Do you love me?' And Peter replies, 'Lord, you know that I love you'. Jesus asks a second time, 'Do you love me?' Again Peter answers, 'But you know that I love you'. A third time, Jesus insists, 'Do you love me more than the others do?' And Peter is troubled. 'Lord, you know everything. You know that I love you.'

Since that day, Christ has been asking every human being on the earth, 'I loved you first. Do you love me?'

There are days when we refuse to listen. The question becomes intolerable, so true it is that no one can love by sheer willpower.

Do we realize sufficiently fully that Christ never obliges any-one to love him? But he, the Living One, is there, poor and unknown, beside each person. He is there, even in the most difficult events, when our life is at its most vulnerable. His love is a presence, not for one fleeting moment, but for ever. This is eternity's love and it opens up for us a way of becoming that lies beyond ourselves. Without this 'beyond', without this 'becoming', hope disappears . . . and the thirst to go forward fades away.

Faced with eternity's love, we can foresee that our response cannot be fleeting, lasting just for a while, until we resume our old life again. But neither can our response be simply an effort of will. That would break some people. Much more, it means surrendering ourselves.

To come before him, with words or without, is to know where our hearts can find rest. It is to respond to him in poverty. Here is the secret incentive for a whole lifetime. Here is the risk of the Gospel. 'O Christ, even if sometimes I do not know anymore whether I love you or not, you know everything and you know that I love you.'

Great happiness is offered to those who take the risk of this love, without calculating the consequences. Once we start seeking happiness as an end in itself, sooner or later we see it vanish. The harder we try to hold on to it, the farther it flees.

Ardent seeker of eternity's love, whoever you are, do you know where your heart can find rest? It is through the very wound within you that he opens the gateway to fullness, in the praising of his love. Surrender yourself, give yourself. There lies the healing for our wounds. And not for ours alone. Already, in him, we are being healed by one another.

1976, A LIFE WE NEVER DARED HOPE FOR

# The Leper's Song

THERE IS a question that rises ceaselessly from the human heart: if God existed, he would not permit wars, injustice, illness and the oppression of even one single human being. If God existed, he would prevent people from doing evil.

In Calcutta, in the course of two visits to a leprosy hospital with Mother Teresa, I saw a leper raise his arms and what remained of his hands and begin to sing these words: 'God has not inflicted a punishment on me. I praise him because my illness has turned into a visit from God.'

This man had realized that suffering does not come from God, it is not the consequence of a misdeed, God is not the author of evil, he is neither a manipulator nor a tormentor of the human conscience.

Listening to the leper's song, I seemed to be hearing Job, that believer long before Christ, on whom trials came pouring down. Job knew that his great suffering was not punishment for a fault. The innocent, devoid of falsehood, can be a victim just as well as the tyrant or the despot with a heart of stone. And one day, like the leper of Calcutta, Job was able to say, 'In my trials, God is seeking for me. I know now that my Redeemer is alive, and my heart is burning within me.'

But why does God not prevent us from doing evil? Because he has not made human beings robots. He has created us in his own image, and that means being free.

When we love a human being with all our hearts, our love desires to leave the loved one free to respond with a similar love, but free as well to refuse.

In the same way God, who loves us with a love beyond words, leaves us free to make a radical choice: free to love but also to refuse love and to reject God; free to spread through the world a leaven of reconciliation or a ferment of injustice; free to love or to hate; free to shine with radiant communion in Christ, but also to tear ourselves away from it and even to destroy other people's thirst for the living God. He leaves us free even to the point of rebelling against him.

But although God leaves us free, he does not look on passively at our distress. He suffers alongside us. Through the Christ who is in agony for every human being on the earth, he visits us, even in the desert of our hearts.

1979, THE WONDER OF A LOVE

# Who Can Condemn Us?

*In church this morning, after I had talked with a number of people, a little girl came up and asked, 'Could you teach me how to confess?' There was a burden weighing on her frail shoulders. How can an eight-year-old child be so imprisoned by anxiety?*

'Who can condemn us, since Jesus is praying for us?' As I listen to young people speaking personally to me, I often wonder what can be the source of the feeling they have of being condemned, of the burden of guilt that has nothing to do with sin.

Sin is a break with Jesus Christ. It means using others, making them victims of oneself.

All human inclinations, the best and the worst, are summed up in each individual, but that is not sin. Yes, every inclination without exception co-exists to a greater or lesser degree in every human being: generosity and selfishness, all the affective tendencies, love and hatred, all in one single being.

When certain young people discover what they are, and have no one to talk to, they can end up believing that they are monsters and they are driven to self-destruction, in extreme cases to suicide.

Who will condemn us? The Gospel knows only one norm: the One who is the most truly human of all, Christ. In spite of our inner contradictions, as we set out again every morning on the way towards Christ, it is with the ultimate hope of becoming transformed to the very likeness of Jesus himself.

Who could condemn? Christ is risen. He condemns no one. He never punishes.

Who could condemn? He is praying in us, offering us the liberation of forgiveness. We in turn become liberators as we forgive, never condemning anyone.

Who could condemn? Even if our own heart condemns us, God is greater than our heart.

1976, A LIFE WE NEVER DARED HOPE FOR

# A Love That Forgives

'WHAT IS forgiveness?' a young Irishman asked me. It is the most unheard of, the most incredible, the most generous of the realities of the Kingdom of God.

How is it then that even certain Christians make use of the weapons of guilt and suspicion, so contrary to the Gospel? They find it difficult to believe that God has forgiven them. They tell themselves, 'God forgives others, but not me'. Caught up in the frenzy of some indefinable guilt, they would like to start by forgiving themselves. Unable to do so, they try to escape from their oppression by accusing other people.

If we had to love God through fear, through dread of punishment, that would never be love. The absolute mark of God, writes Saint John, the mystic, is that he is love. And his love, like all love, is first and foremost trust and forgiveness.

Christ does not want us drunk with guilt, but simply filled to overflowing with forgiveness and trust.

Sometimes you ask me where is the source, where is the joy of hoping.
I will answer you.

All your past, even the moment that has just gone by, is already swallowed up, drowned, with Christ in the water of your baptism.

Do not look back. That is part of Christian freedom. The one thing that is interesting is running to meet what is still to come.

Give up looking back. Not in order to be irresponsible. If you have wounded your neighbour, are you going to leave them lying by the roadside? Are you going to refuse reconciliation, refuse to pour oil on their wound?

Give up looking back. Not in order to forget the best of your past. It is for you to celebrate the moments when God has passed through your life, to call to mind your inner liberations.

You will say that nobody can forget the devastations of sin. Tenacious, stabbing regrets remain.

If your imagination brings back destructive memories from the past, at least be aware that God, for his part, takes no account of them.

Do you understand? One of the greatest risks in living Christ for others is forgiveness. To forgive and forgive again, that is what wipes out the past and plunges you into the present moment.

Christian, you bear the name of Christ. For you every moment can become fullness of life.

The word love is often abused. It is so easily said. Living out a love that forgives is another matter.

You cannot forgive out of self-interest, in order to change the other person. That would be a miserable calculation which has nothing to do with the free gift of love. You can only forgive because of Christ.

You will dare to pray with Jesus his last prayer, 'Father, forgive them, they do not know what they are doing'. And spontaneously this second prayer will spring up, 'Father, forgive me, so often I do not know what I am doing either'.

Forgiving means refusing to take into account what the other person will do with your forgiveness.

Forgiving. There lies the secret incentive that will make you too a witness to a future that is different.

1982, AND YOUR DESERTS SHALL FLOWER

# From Doubt To A Fine Human Hope

*Since we came back from Calcutta, my heart has been full of images: the eyes of tiny infants, children living in the streets, the look of young women lepers, ravaged by inner loneliness.*

*After spending some time sharing in the life of an Asian slum, how can we possibly find some of the conflicts in Europe other than ludicrous? The divisions between Christians, old or new, the misunderstandings between generations, don't these look like much ado about nothing? Do the challenges of the Gospel not ring out more clearly in surroundings of great poverty, like the neighbourhood in Calcutta where we were staying?*

*Could the Gospel be lived out more clearly in conditions of extreme poverty? Yet in the northern hemisphere there is a thirst for God and it is even becoming stronger.*

*No, life in Europe has nothing ludicrous about it. But seen from Asia, the northern hemisphere looks as if it were crossed by vast tracts of spiritual desert. These deserts are inhabited by boredom, disillusionment, and by a diffuse doubt that leads to scepticism.*

In the northern continents, sometimes just under the surface, there can be a fundamental loneliness, of people who have been totally abandoned. Europe and North America have their 'homes for the dying' just as much as Asia does, only they are invisible. There are young people, faced with an uncertain future, who even wonder why they were born. When they no longer see the meaning of life, they let themselves drift downhill until mere survival is the only goal they have left.

How can we find fulfilment in God, surrounded as we are by all-pervasive doubt? How can we move from doubt to hope in God, or at least, for non-believers, from doubt to a fine human hope?

On my journeys to Eastern Europe in recent years, I have had the chance to discover that, although deserts of doubt stretch right across the northern hemisphere, they are perceived in a different way by young Christians in the East from those in the West.

In the East, circumstances lead some young Christians, not all of them, of course, to pay more attention than ever to the essential elements of the faith. They find no answer to the doubt all around them except in a far-reaching commitment of their lives.

Concerning the search for God in the West, some young people — not all — seem to be driven to prove that they are 'emancipated'. As consumers, they have so many possibilities at their disposal, not just of material goods but of leisure and of culture itself, that they find self-fulfilment only in what enthrals them. Dialogue with a view to understanding God sometimes becomes chatter about everything and nothing.

For anyone seeking fulfilment in Christ, the present situation arouses uneasiness. In both East and West, doubt can attack believers like a kind of subtle, invisible persecution, until they may even begin to think that they have been abandoned by God and his Christ.

In a civilization where doubt is all pervasive, Christians are deeply affected when they hear it said that their faith is only a projection of themselves. The world of doubt becomes corrosive through analyses that are exclusively cerebral and which mean death for the heart.

The temptation of doubt puts our trust in God to the test. It can purify as gold is purified by fire. It can also cast a human being down into the bottom of a pit. But there always remains a light shining from above. The darkness is never total. It never invades the whole person completely for God is present even in the darkness.

When people who are racked by the trial of doubt want to live the Gospel, they allow themselves to be brought to life day after day by the trust of God. It is there that life finds meaning again.

The meaning of life cannot be gathered from the clouds or from opinions. It draws its nourishment from trust. God sets his trust on every human being like a breath of his Spirit.

One of the essential marks of the Gospel is that in return God invites human beings to place their trust in a Person who has come out of the grave and who is alive. Faith is not an opinion, it is an attitude. Believers welcome the Risen Lord and they too become fully alive, not half-dead. In the early days of the Church, Irenaeus of Lyons, a Christian of the third generation after Christ — he had known Polycarp who had himself been a disciple of John the Evangelist — wrote, 'The glory of God is a human being fully alive. The life of a human being is the vision of God.'

Everywhere in the world, large numbers of young people intent on prayer would like to devote their energies to some generous project. Deep in their hearts there is a sense of the universal, a yearning for solidarity with the whole human family, often with its most deprived members. When opportunities are offered, they come running from every side. But when such opportunities do not arise, some of them drift into excruciating discouragement, the supreme temptation of our time.

For these young people, the future seems like a dead end.

They feel that the older generation is ready to give them material things, pocket money, salaries and unemployment benefits, but not to offer them a share in building society. Since they take so little part in decision-making for the ongoing life of society and for peace, as well as for the building of the Church, they withdraw into themselves. Their abilities are wasting away in obsessive boredom.

Young people of all the nations of the earth are aspiring to build peace. They are ready to stand together and be a leaven of peace, right there in situations where the human family is being torn apart, be it in the East, the West, the North or the South.

Are they really aware of it? These young people have all that is necessary to overturn the inevitability of hatred, war and violence, to restore courage to those who were at the mercy of diffuse, subtle doubt, and to replace disillusionment with a fine human hope.

1982, AND YOUR DESERTS SHALL FLOWER

# Living God's Today

PEOPLE WHO strive to surrender themselves to God body and soul let themselves be built up from within on the basis of a few simple truths from the Gospel. Truths which at one time or another have touched them to the core. Why not summarize them briefly so that they can be called to mind at any moment?

The fruit of much thought, matured slowly and worked out over a long period of time, this summary most often takes shape in the midst of life's struggles. Once we have found it, it can carry us forward our whole life long.

This does not mean a great many words, but a few essential Gospel values that are concise and clear enough for us to return to them again and again. If we forget them for a time, we can return to them again the very moment that they come to mind.

For those who are patient and who consent to this necessary process of maturing, the day comes when the core of their personality has been fashioned without their realizing it.

Those who surrender themselves to the Spirit of the living God do not fix their gaze on their own progress or backsliding. Like someone who is walking along a narrow ridge, they go straight forward, forgetting what lies behind. They make no attempt to measure the minute changes that are taking place within. They do not know how, but the seed sprouts and grows, by day and by night.

If there is a Christian form of discipline, it is based neither on will-power nor on a morality of things to be given up. Far from being an end in itself, it is a humble response to a love.

If it is a good thing to pray at fixed times, it is out of love, not because God obliges us to do so. God never forces our hearts.

There is no need to rack our brains to know what sacrifices to impose on ourselves. It is much better to accomplish simply what is necessary in the present moment. There are times when our hearts prefer idealistic demands to peacefully following the way that is set out before us.

There are days when it is hard to keep going. But without perseverance our commitment wastes away. Remaining faithful even more in times of dryness than when faith breaks spontaneously into prayer. Keeping in mind the times that were filled with a Presence.

The only remedy for formalism and routine lies in remaining true to a resolution we have made, and in this way, fervour and adoration will spring up once again.

To recover vital energy, at each new dawn take hold of the coming day. God is preparing something brand new in each one of us.

Living God's today. That is the most important thing. And tomorrow will be another 'God's today'.

Finding fulfilment in the present moment. Anyone fixed on tomorrow forfeits today.

Enthusiasm, serene joy, yes. Not euphoria. That is only a flash in the pan.

'You who give food to the birds of the air and who make the lilies of the field to grow, enable us to rejoice in the things with which you fill us, and may that be enough for us.'

1985, A HEART THAT TRUSTS

# A Continuous Festival

*One day, one of the young brothers discovered this saying of St Athanasius, 'The Risen Christ makes human life a continuous festival'. When the brother first told me these words, I did not say anything but I thought, 'That "continuous" is a bit exaggerated'.*

*Today however, I believe that St Athanasius knew why he said what he did. Our existence as Christians means constantly living the paschal mystery: a succession of little deaths that are followed by the beginnings of a resurrection. From there on, every way lies open and our lives can go forward, making use of what is good and of what is not so good. A festive spirit re-surfaces even in moments when we hardly know what is happening to us, even in the hardest trial of all, when a close relationship breaks up. The heart is broken but not hardened. It begins to live again.*

*How can we kindle a festive spirit within us? First of all by consenting to our own humanity. Because of Christ nothing is ever lost. He gathers up everything to such an extent that when we awake each morning, the spirit of praise can predominate. Whatever may be the difficult events that present themselves during the day, we are enlivened from within and the events are* modified and transformed; people who were crushed are raised up. The spirit of festival is not the result of an artificial 'high'. Festival is built up. In life's monotony, little by little, a hidden brightness becomes manifest.

Meals are a way of renewing festival. Do you know how the brothers and I travel sometimes? When we go by train we take our food with us. If it is evening, we turn out the lights, light a great big candle and invite the others who are there to eat with us. In this way we can rejoice not only among ourselves but with the people around us too.

The older I grow, the more my heart seeks happiness in the witnesses to whom I turn. I often read a few words of John XXIII. I loved him, and it was mutual. I need his face and I trust in his prayer, since he is in God's eternity.

Faces count even more than words for remaining in a festive spirit. They express friendship, and friendship is the face of Christ. Nothing is more beautiful than a face that has been made transparent by a whole life of struggle and combat. There are only beautiful faces, be they sad or radiant. My life consists in discerning in other people what is ravaging them and what is making them joyful; it lies in communion in the suffering and in the joy of others.

All my life since I was very young, my desire has been never to condemn anyone. For me the essential has always been to understand the other person fully. When I do manage to understand somebody, that is already a festival.

1971, FESTIVAL WITHOUT END

# Letting Christ Transfigure The Shadows

OUTSIDE THE light of Christ, the shadows fall. They envelop us. This is true for everyone, but we feel it more deeply at certain moments of our lives or at certain periods in history.

The light of the transfiguration of Christ means that the work of the resurrection has already begun in us, today.

In one of his letters, the apostle Peter, who was present at the event, gives us the meaning of the transfiguration. He shows us a fundamental attitude of the Christian life.

We are in the night. In the midst of the darkness, there shines a source of light. It is ours to focus our eyes on that light 'until the day begins to dawn and the morning star rises in our heart' (2 Peter 1.19).

Why should we go searching far away for what is so close at hand? There are times when we would like to do without faith and patience; we would like marvels and miracles, signs plain to see. It is ours instead to persevere in keeping our eyes fixed on the light until the morning star rises in our hearts. And as we remain before God, we can see everything henceforth in the light of Christ.

Look at every human being in that light. Know that in each

person, even in those who do not confess Christ, there shines a reflection of the Creator's image. Our neighbour is not necessarily the person we find congenial. She or he is the human being that we find lying by the roadside, wounded by life. Our neighbour is not just a person for whom we feel immediate friendship but is someone who deserves more than anyone else to be looked at through the eyes of Christ himself, precisely because she or he means nothing to us.

Look at Christians in that light. See them first and foremost as bearers of Christ. Give up complaining about all that may be negative in them and consider only the light that has been placed within them, the gifts of God. Nothing renews us more than discovering the living hope that fills one of God's witnesses.

Look at ourselves in the light of Christ, too. Instead of being brought to a standstill because there is evil and limitations within us — and there always will be — learn how to lay down all these burdens. Some people find the means of handing over everything in the sacrament of reconciliation. When we have received forgiveness, it is essential to root our lives in it straight away, because we cannot live from our guilt feelings but from Christ who lives within us.

Look at and consider all of life, all of creation, in this light, since in the beginning the whole of creation was placed in the fullness of God.

A plant that is not turned towards the light withers away. How can believers allow an interior life to grow within them if they forget to look at the light of God and concentrate only on the shadows?

The apostles were led apart from the others on the mountain top and given a glimpse of what was to be theirs on the day when they would be one with Christ in God (Matthew 17.1–8).

Little by little, Christ transforms and transfigures all the rebellious and contradictory forces in us, the other self that is still alive and over which at times our will has no control. Our troubled, uninhabited, unbelieving depths are transfigured. By a slow working out of the life of the Holy Spirit within us, perceptible or not, what was dark becomes clear and is peacefully taken up in God. God alone reaches the unreachable, that rebel will that does not accomplish the good it wants, but does the wrong it does not want. Such a transfiguration is the beginning of the resurrection, right here on the earth.

It is possible to assure certain people who are convinced that their lives are failures that, in the heart of God, nothing is lost. Christians like St John of the Cross and St Teresa of Avila started a new life quite late on, yet they have led countless women and men to Christ, and they speak of the fire that was kindled with all the dry wood of their past.

For those who are marked by suffering and by the cross of Christ, the day will come when they will be able to burn with the flame that is fed with all their past life. They will know that in God nothing is lost. Christ does not come to destroy flesh and blood. He does not break what is in us. He has not come to abolish but to fulfil. When darkness gathers, his love is a fire.

In every man and in every woman there is a wound, inflicted by failures, humiliations, bad conscience. Perhaps it was caused at a time when we needed infinite understanding and nobody was there to give it.

If we complain about this wound, it becomes a torment, an aggressive force turned against ourselves and against others, often against those who are closest to us.

Transfigured by Christ, it is changed into a focus of energy, into a source of creativity where communion, friendship and understanding burst forth.

As the light of Christ is at work in the heart of our inner nights, so too it is active in the obscurity of the world. In this way, God is taking humanity upon himself: living in the midst of the human family, Christians are bearers of the Spirit of the Risen Christ; with great discretion, they communicate the presence of God himself.

As the apostles contemplate the Risen Christ, they want to remain there in the dazzling light. They know that they are experiencing one of the most important moments of their lives. But they must come down from the mountain top.

This is true for every believer. We have to come down from the mountain in order to shine with the radiance of God, to be bearers of peace and reconciliation in the divisions of the Christian family and in the divisions that are tearing the human family apart. We must do this so that, by the light of Christ within us, even people who cannot believe may be led, though they may not understand how, towards the hope of God.

1981, THE LETTER FROM TAIZÉ

# PEACE OF HEART IN ALL THINGS

# The Christ Who Accompanies Us

*Hong Kong. We have been offered a place to stay on the South China Sea, among poor people who are living in junks in a 'floating neighbourhood'. On the edge of the area, one of the families is about to move on to a better place and they have agreed to leave us their shack, built on tall piles driven into the water.*

*Here, the 'street' is the water, with little boats going back and forth all the time. Our shack is made of bits and pieces of used planks and crates. When the tide rises, it sways gently. There is no electricity. Drinking water has to be brought in by boat.*

*The reserved Sacrament has been placed below the icon of Christ. In the poverty of this place, there is now a corner of rare beauty. We are drawn there irresistibly to pray.*

*Some workmen from a neighbouring building-site share our meal. They come from mainland China and return there regularly. They say they have never had an invitation like this one before. They can see us praying every day. One of them points a finger to the sky to say he understands what that means.*

*Why have we come to share the life of the destitute on the South China Sea? It is not through personal taste or natural inclination; it is to introduce the most trying conditions of human life into our own lives. We are all getting on extremely well together. An ocean of goodness shines on these people's faces.*

*These non-believers are inhabited by a presence. Surrounded as we are by this Chinese population, we are overwhelmed by the conviction that every creature is visited by the Spirit of God, wherever they may be. In the West too, so many men and women are experiencing the silence of God. The night seems dark and they wonder, 'But where is God?' During this time here on the South China Sea, it is becoming so clear that the silence of God exists only on the level of appearances. Christ is standing at the door, knocking. By his mysterious presence as the Risen One, he stands close by each one of us, including those who do not even know his name.*

On the evening of his resurrection, Jesus accompanied two of his disciples who were on their way to Emmaus, but at that moment they did not recognize that it was Jesus.

There are times in our lives too when we are unable to grasp that he is walking along with us. Yet whether we recognize him or not, whether we sense his presence or refuse it, he is there, even when we have no possible reason for hoping so. He is praying within us in the silence of our hearts, in an unvoiced prayer.

At other times, we understand that he is with us and we want to talk to him. Then our prayer is explicit. 'Show us the way', we ask. And he replies, 'I am here'. Again we say, 'Listen, listen to my prayer, the prayer of a child'. And our praying remains simple throughout our lives, like the prayers of childhood.

Why should we force our lips to formulate prayers at times when the whole of our being objects? If mind and heart can temporarily express nothing, the prayer of the body takes over, to express our intention or our surrender to the silence of God. The Gospel of Luke comes to an end with the disciples bowed low, praying with their foreheads touching the ground.

In everyday living there is a whole language that comes from us for communicating with God. This in itself may not yet be prayer but it is the self already on its way to being unified. Sowing wheat in the field, leaving for work in the morning, caring for the sick, listening to others, writing, studying to become qualified, all of these can become a language with God.

In the course of our days and our nights, there are things we accomplish because of Christ, and these things become prayer: forgiveness, reconciliation, a struggle to remain faithful in marriage or in celibacy offered to God. These signs and many others are a language that we address to Christ. They are accomplished for his sake and they show him our love.

And days will come again when the fire of a passion for God will show itself in an overflowing heart, in boundless imagination and in a song that is sung over and over again.

In this way, times of ardent searching for God and times of intense everyday activity gradually come together. Prayer and life meet and form one single reality.

Prayer, whether it is explicit or not, brings peace and rest to the core of our being.

Knowing where to find rest for our hearts means grasping a reality that is hidden from our eyes: Christ is accompanying us by his mysterious presence. And from then on our burdened hearts begin to live again. They start to sing again, sometimes even without a sound, 'The breath of your loving has visited me. I am no longer marking time. I am accompanying you.'

1979, THE WONDER OF A LOVE

# The Fire Of A Passion For God

*Spending a few moments in the pottery. On a blackboard where the young brothers who work there are in the habit of writing up a quotation, there are these words, 'Your love, O Christ, has wounded my soul. I go forward singing your praises.' Are the young brothers the authors of such a profound thought? No. It was written in old age by John Climacus in the seventh century. He had entered the monastery of Sinai at the age of fifteen and he came to realize that a passion for Christ is lived with a person's entire being, body and spirit.*

When people are seeking the Risen Christ, they are dealing with the realities of the Kingdom of God. These cannot be measured; they have no beginning and no end. Prayer opens up a boundless communion among countless believers. Through prayer, a relationship is created with the eternity of God. If, in the flash of a moment, we are able to experience an encounter with Christ, it is a moment that passes just as quickly as it comes, and sometimes we only realize it after the event: 'Yes! He was here, it was him.'

Rare indeed are ecstasies or mystical visions. The miracle

lies elsewhere. 'We have never seen Christ, but we love him' (cf. 1 Peter 1.8).

This reality is astounding and it is almost beyond the grasp of the human mind: Christ dwells in us, but also we dwell in him. Through the Holy Spirit, he loves in us, in our heart of hearts. That is a miracle.

Here is what I would like to say to people who are anxious about the poor quality of their praying:

Prayer is not a personal feat. When you pray alone, sometimes it seems as if clouds had come down between God and you. These clouds have names: rebellion, frustration, the feeling of being unworthy or incapable, the loss of self-esteem. So many subjective realities can raise up a wall between him and you.

When you forget his presence, are you going to waste your time in complaining about your forgetfulness? Surrender yourself instead to confident trust. The Risen Christ is to be found everywhere, in the street, at work, in church. Whatever your age and your condition, you can tell him everything, like a child; all that imprisons you, all that hurts you, all that is burdening many others, both near and far. He will clear a way through. And you will never be bored in this face-to-face dialogue.

In order to pray at all times, day and night, and even when hard at work, do not hesitate to repeat over and over again a phrase or a simple chant: 'Jesus, my joy, my hope and my life', 'In you, Jesus, joy, simplicity and mercy'; 'Mon âme se repose en paix sur Dieu seul' (My soul finds rest and peace in God alone); 'Bleibet hier und wachet mit mir, wachet und betet' (Stay with me, keep watch with me, watching and praying); 'Nada te turbe, sólo Dios basta' (Let nothing disturb you, God alone is enough).

If there are times when you are unable to pray at all, then it is still possible for you to entrust yourself to the prayer of someone else, and that someone could well be a person who is in the evening of their life.

In a technological civilization, we are often keenly aware of the break between prayer and work. When struggle and contemplation appear to be in competition, as if we had to opt for one against the other, the opposition between them can tear apart the very foundations of the soul.

A life of communion with God is not lived out in dreams that hover between heaven and earth. Far from forgetting others, such a life is rooted in real-life situations. It takes upon itself the contradictions of the human condition, as well as those of contemporary society, with its prevailing characteristics: the fascination with means of power, success at all costs, an atmosphere of doubt that certainly has to be reckoned with.

Sometimes, in their understandable desire to go out and meet a secularized world, local Christian communities and groups have believed that they even had to secularize their worship. But then the depths of the human being are no longer being touched. Common prayer can never be a monologue where, although people think they are speaking to God, in fact each person is simply trying to put their own ideas across to others. An act of common prayer means that everyone, including the person who is presiding, is turned towards the living God.

Prayer is a serene force that is at work in human beings, stirring them, never allowing them to fall asleep or to close their eyes to evil, to wars, to all that threatens or attacks the weak of this world.

Those who are following in the steps of Christ are living both for other people and for God. They are not seeking to separate prayer and action.

1982, AND YOUR DESERTS SHALL FLOWER

# A Life From Elsewhere

PEOPLE WHO pray have a guiding star. Like a hidden, invisible pole, it draws them on. Frequently they are obliged to feel their way, but the goal they have in view fills their whole being, leading them along.

Step by step they discover that they have been created to be the dwelling place of Another. As they begin to listen to what is happening in their heart of hearts, they understand that they are unique. Through their poor praying, they are being touched to the core; they are becoming someone else for other people.

Prayer is both struggle and surrender. It is also waiting: waiting for a way through, waiting for the walls of our inner resistance to break down. Just as we do, Christ in his earthly life experienced times of intense patience.

Prayer is an astonishing thing. It propels us elsewhere, out of ourselves. We can recognize Christ in our neighbour, and he is always alive within ourselves, but he is elsewhere too, present in his own right.

Prayer is always poor and we who are living it will be poor servants to the very end. Prayer will always exceed our powers.

Words are unfit to describe it. In prayer there lies something beyond what we are, beyond our own words.

Coherence in language is most important for all of us. So when we approach this fluid realm where everything seems to happen in ways that cannot be described, it is easy to understand that many people's first reaction is a bit like fear. It has been like that from the very beginnings of Christian history. 'We do not know how to pray, but the Holy Spirit comes to the help of our weakness and prays in us' (Romans 8.26). Down through the centuries, prayer never changes in its essence, but, as history unfolds or at different moments of our lives, it takes on different forms.

Some people pray without words. Everything is wrapped in a great silence.

Other people use many words to express themselves. In the sixteenth century, Teresa of Avila, a woman of great courage and realism, wrote about prayer in this way. 'When I speak to the Lord, I often do not know what I am saying. And the soul is so beside itself that I can see no difference between it and God. Love forgets itself and says foolish things.'

Others find in the liturgy or in common prayer the joy of heaven on earth, a fulfilment . . .

There are people who repeat over and over again a few words that they have learned to stammer. Through this prayer of the poor people that we all are, a unity of their personality is built up within them. They repeat the angel's greeting to Mary: 'Hail, Mary, full of grace . . .'. These may be the only words they have left when they are caught off their guard by the suffering they see. Or else, audibly or not, to the rhythm of their breathing, they murmur the prayer of the Name of Jesus. To all appearances, the endless repetition of the same words has no spontaneity. And yet, after a long time of waiting, life comes surging up within, a fullness, the Holy Spirit's unsettling presence.

There are still others who practically never experience any awareness of a presence within them. Their whole life long, they are in expectation and that is the fire that lies behind their searching. For them, contemplation is a struggle. It does not bring immediate fullness flooding over them. It does not arouse any spontaneous outburst of feeling for Christ.

The ways of prayer are many. Some people follow one, others follow them all. There are moments of clear certainty: Christ is there, speaking within us. But there are other moments when he is Silence, a distant Stranger. No one is privileged in prayer.

In its infinite diversity, prayer leads all of us into a life that does not come from ourselves but from elsewhere.

1976, A LIFE WE NEVER DARED HOPE FOR

# The Gateways Of Praise

One day, someone dear to me was describing a whole inner conflict: 'I have known what it is to be tempted by self-analysis, with all its question marks, its incessant 'who-are-you's and its endless 'why's. This kind of questioning can sometimes lead to vanity, but more often than not the result is sadness, shame and even self-contempt. So I kept turning over the soil of my being, working it over in an attempt to make it more and more beautiful, until I ended up by making the beauty of the soil a goal in itself, forgetting that the goal is to sow a seed of the Gospel in it.

'I knew the words of Isaiah, "You shall call your gateways 'praise' ".

'But my gateways were called introspection, anguish and scruple. I had written on them, "I am no more worthy to be called your son". These are narrow gates that do not open outwards at all, but inwards, towards the lower depths of the self.

'From now on, I shall call my gateways "praise". These are gates that open wide towards the outside world, towards him who is beyond things and beyond myself.'

*When introspection and self-analysis turn people in on themselves, what destruction that brings! Who will open the gateways of praise for them?*

*Shortly before he died in 1942, Miguel Hernández, a political prisoner in southern Spain, revealed something like a secret:*

> *Open in me, Love,*
> *the gates of the perfect wound;*
> *Open, to release*
> *all the anguish;*
> *Open, see, it is coming,*
> *the breath of your word.*

*Through the gateways of praise will pass both deathly anguish and songs unending. God will set his mark on the wounds themselves. They will no longer be torment, but energy for communion.*

To want a life with no contradictions, no shocks, no opposition, and with no criticism, is to want to live in the clouds. So when turmoil comes, inside ourselves, in the Church or in society, two ways are offered to us:

Either pain and anguish change into bitterness and, as we groan under the crushing burden, we become rooted to the spot and all is lost.

Or else pain and sadness find an outlet in the praise of his love, and this draws us out of our passiveness and enables us to deal with events as they come.

1976, A LIFE WE NEVER DARED HOPE FOR

# In A Breath Of Silence

NEARLY THREE thousand years ago, a believer called Elijah had the intuition that God speaks to us in the desert and that a silent trust lies at the beginning of everything.

His people were giving themselves over to all kinds of beliefs, of every form imaginable. Faith was disappearing. These tendencies occur again and again in human history: anything but the living God.

Elijah does his utmost to make himself understood but he does not succeed. Deeply discouraged and at the end of his resources, he asks God for death.

One day, Elijah is called to go up into the desert of Mount Sinai in order to listen to God. On Sinai, a hurricane arises, then an earthquake, then a raging fire. But Elijah realizes that God is not in these outbursts of nature.

It is perhaps one of the first times in history that such a crystal-clear intuition was written down: God does not impose his will by violence. God does not speak through terrifying acts of power. Today as yesterday, God is not the author of wars, disasters, misfortunes, or of any human suffering.

Then, on Sinai, everything becomes quiet. Elijah hears God

in a kind of whisper. And the striking fact dawns upon him: often the voice of God comes in a breath of silence.

God never imposes his will upon anyone.

God does not ask us to force manifestations of the Spirit. That would mean lighting fireworks that blaze up and then die away immediately. People who play this game think they are in touch with God when really it is only a projection of their own ego. Trying to draw others into forced experiences of the Spirit of God would be leading them into illusion, and even into a bottomless pit.

Today as yesterday, God never stops speaking. Often his voice is heard as a breath of silence.

Could God's apparent silence be concealing a communion, the kind of communion where 'deep calls to deep'? The human spirit is unfathomable, an abyss! But God is there already.

Happy the pure in heart! They discover, even beneath the silences of the Gospel, that the most amazing mystery of all is the continuing presence of the Risen Christ offered to every single one of us.

Peace of heart in all things. If our prayer is sometimes nothing but poor stammerings, that does not matter. The realities of the Kingdom of God cannot be measured. In one sense, perhaps it is better that way. Let us be glad that in this way God gives us humility.

And God understands all human languages. He understands our words. But he understands our silences too. And silence is sometimes everything in prayer.

It is not a question of achieving inner silence at all costs, by creating a kind of nothingness within, through stifling imagination and thought.

During prayer, thoughts and images cross the mind. Perhaps they are necessary for keeping an even keel within. To people who catch themselves thinking, 'My thoughts are wandering, my heart is not concentrated', the Gospel answers, 'God is greater than your heart'.

It is useless to impose methods on ourselves or on others in order to force inner silence. Knowing certain principles of posture or breath control is sometimes necessary. But from there to turning these into a recipe or wanting to propagate one's own method, there is a world of difference.

When prayer is subjected to a technique, we are building with ourselves as the starting point. Every system, including mysticism, runs the risk of encountering a God manufactured out of human projections.

Happy the pure in heart. They will see God. In each one of us, the Kingdom within has no beginning and no end.

1985, A Heart That Trusts

# The Silence of Contemplation

PRAYER, descending into the depths of God, is not there to make us better inside. Praying, not with an eye on some kind of usefulness, but in order to create with Christ a communion of human beings who are totally free.

When we strive to give expression in words to this communion, we have conscious prayers. Yet our understanding can express only the outer surface of ourselves. Very soon it comes up short . . . and silence takes over, to the point of seeming to mean that God is not there.

Instead of getting stuck on the barrenness of silence, remember that it opens out into unheard of possibilities of creativity. In the world that underlies the human personality, Christ is praying, more than we can imagine. Compared with the vastness of this secret prayer of Christ within us, the prayer we express in words seems very little.

The silence of contemplation! In every one of us, there lie unknown depths of doubt, of violence, of secret distress . . . and also chasms of guilt, of things unacknowledged, to the point that we sense an immense void gaping beneath our feet. We do not know where the impulses seething within us come from; perhaps from some ancestral or genetic memory. So, trusting like a child, let Christ pray within us, and one day these depths will be inhabited.

With time, out of contemplation there arises happiness. And this happiness is a wellspring of our struggle for and with the human family. It is courage. It is energy for taking risks. It is overflowing gladness.

1973, STRUGGLE AND CONTEMPLATION

# Praying With Mary And The Apostles

*For almost twenty-five years now, my brothers and I have been going back and forth, visiting the Christians in the countries of Eastern Europe. It was a brother who is now in the eternity of God who was the first to have this intuition. I myself have been able to go often, and just before leaving on one of these visits, I received this letter from the people I was going to meet:*

*'We are expecting a message from you, not just for ourselves, but for all the Christians throughout the world who are undergoing trials. Here is our contribution towards the preparation of your message:*

*'Our situation resembles that of the apostles and Mary just after the death of Christ. Jesus had suffered. He was dead. The disciples were bewildered and filled with fear.*

*'But after a time of despair, we, like them, have understood: Christ is risen! Fear and despair are already behind us. We are no longer completely bewildered. Yet, like the apostles, our possibilities are limited.*

*'We are aware intuitively that all that has happened has come about so that Jesus could send his Spirit. It is only a preparation for a new springtime of the Church. The important*

thing for us now is to recognize the specific grace that Jesus is offering us in our situation, to pray with Mary and the apostles, in a prayer that the Holy Spirit is communicating to our hearts.

'Yes, even people who have no means, who have no outward possibilities at all, can do this: in small communities, with their sisters and brothers, with Mary and the apostles, they can pray in hopeful waiting on the Holy Spirit.

'That is our vocation at the present time. To pray that the people of God may become a contemplative people who live lives that are deeply rooted in the Spirit of the Risen Christ.'

1981, THE LETTER FROM WARSAW

# Moments When God Is Everything

TO GO ON waiting for God, in passionate longing, is not beyond our ability.

Contemplation is often perceived as the opposite to action. It is seen as passivity, or a flight from the real struggles.

Yet facts speak for themselves. Some Christians give themselves so generously. Their commitment entails great personal risk. Yet they hold fast to the very wellsprings of contemplation.

What are we to understand by contemplation? Quite simply the attitude in which our whole being is totally seized by the wonder of a presence. When we understand the vast reality of the beauty of things intellectually, in one sense we have indeed been seized by it all, but that is only partial. It is the whole of our being, emotions and all, that is seized by the reality of the love of God.

Some people are in the grip of the subjective experience of the silence of God, as if the presence of God were bound to our perception and to what we feel.

Can they have forgotten? God is there too in the times that enthusiasm evaporates and all apparent feeling vanishes.

God says: Before you were born, I dreamt of you.

When we realize that God loved us first, even before we loved him, we can only tear aside the veil under which we have been hiding.

The day will come when each one of us will know and perhaps even say, 'No, God did not go away. I was the one who was absent. God was with me all the time.'

And then come moments when God is everything.

1985, A HEART THAT TRUSTS

# YOU ASPIRE TO
# FOLLOW CHRIST

# All Or Nothing

*One of the questions we are asked most often is, 'Why are so many young people from every continent coming to Taizé?' We do not really know why. God will tell us on the day when we meet him face to face in the life of eternity.*

*Every evening, winter and summer, when a few of us stay on in church to listen to the young people one at a time, one of the things that concern us is to understand what lies 'underneath' their hearts, what is holding them captive? And then there appears an even more important necessity, namely, what are their particular gifts? And how can they discover them?*

*We know that they have not come here as tourists. If they had, then they would have come to the wrong address. The great majority have come with one and the same question: how can I understand God? How can I know what God wants for me?*

*If they have come here, in their thirst for the living God, it is to question themselves in the silence of their hearts, in order to seek to follow Christ.*

As you aspire to follow the Risen Christ, how can you recognize if you have encountered him?

Rather than trying to feel his presence, do you know how to discern God in the simple events of life and put into practice every day the suggestions that he is placing in you?

By what sign can you recognize that you have encountered Christ? When you are led, irresistibly, to leave everything behind, to leave yourself behind, not knowing where you are headed. You have encountered him when, try as you may to stop your ears, his words ring out within you, 'You, come and follow me'.

Long before Christ, an Old Testament believer wrote, 'My Child, if you aspire to serve the Lord, prepare yourself for trials. Be sincere of heart, and be steadfast' (Ecclesiasticus 2.1).

Choosing Christ is a matter of all or nothing. There is no middle ground. Will you go to the point of bearing in your body the marks of Jesus and the burning of his love? These are recognizable in you when you are able to tell him, 'You loved me first. You are my joy, my essential love, may that be enough for me.'

If you are seeking to follow him right to the end, however much it may cost you, then prepare yourself, poor as you are, to experience the struggles of the faithfulness of each day. Through these small events, you are linked to an immense reality. And in this way, humanity filled with understanding for everyone and a heart as wide as the world will be fashioned within you.

Choosing Christ! He confronts us with an alternative. 'Whoever wants to save their life will lose it. Whoever gives their life for the love of me will find it.' Yet he does not impose the choice. He leaves everyone free to choose him or to reject him. He never forces us. Simply, for two thousand years, gentle and humble of heart, he has been standing at the door of every human heart, knocking.

When it seems that our ability to respond to him has disappeared, we can only call out, 'Give me the gift of giving myself, of resting in you, O Christ, body and spirit'.

Choosing Christ means walking on one road only, not on two roads at the same time. Those who want to follow Christ and to follow themselves at the same time end up following their own shadow, in pursuit of reputation or prestige.

The day will come again when you whisper:
'In my longing to live nothing but the one essential, I remember you, the Risen Christ. My heart, my mind, my body are like dry ground, thirsting for you. I had forgotten you, but all the time I kept on loving you. And you shower on me a love called forgiveness; you make me someone who is fully alive.'

As you aspire to follow the Risen Christ, by what other sign can you recognize that you have met him? When the inner struggles you wage in order to follow him, the trials which can even cause a flood of tears to flow within, when this whole combat, far from making you hard and bitter, is transfigured and becomes a source of new energy.

Such a transfiguration is the beginning of the resurrection, right here on earth. It is a revolution that is taking place within us, it is living the passover with Jesus, it is a continual passing from death to life.

In this inner revolution, all that could devastate our being, loneliness, feelings of uselessness, everything that otherwise would shatter the fibres of the soul, all of these no longer block the way forward, but instead lead to a breakthrough from anguish to trust, from resignation to creative enthusiasm.

You aspire to follow the Lord, so do not fear to enter into a passover with Christ. When you hear him say to you, 'Come, follow me', you will be surprised to find yourself answering:
'I have recognized you. I would like to be close to you for you listen to the simple words I stammer in prayer — you, the Christ of glory, risen within everyone who is seeking for you.

'And I would like to be able to accompany you even in your agony for humanity, for you are close to whoever is in distress and to whoever is striving for the good of other people.

'To put my thrust in you, to make my heart steadfast, I shall go so far, violently if need be, as to hook my heart on to the heart of God. I have clearly understood; only the violent take hold of the realities of the Kingdom of heaven.'

Being sustained entirely by his trust is love at its purest, not an illusory love that is content with words, but a trusting love that takes hold of the whole being at every moment, a love strong as death.

1979, THE WONDER OF A LOVE

# The Risk Of Living From Him

YOU ARE aspiring to follow Christ. You can only encounter him by placing your trust in him. There is no other way.

But how can you trust him and follow him in a lifelong commitment when you are so afraid of making a mistake or, later on, of having made a mistake in the past?

To prepare yourself to say this 'yes' and then to live it, you need someone with whom you can talk about yourself. Not just anybody. Otherwise you will look for someone who is inclined towards what are easy options for you, and these will never make you a creator. You can speak about what lies buried in your heart only to someone who has a gift of discernment and is experienced, who can read what lies beneath the contradictions of the human personality.

People who exercise this ministry of listening have no method and no theory. They do not give the same answer to everyone. Everything depends on each person's basic gift.

To one person, they will have to say, 'Leave everything, right away. Otherwise you will be running away from God.' To someone else, just as eager to follow Christ, they will say instead, 'To commit your whole life in God, first acquire the necessary qualifications in a profession, so as to be able to serve others. Interrupting your professional training now would be taking the easy way out.'

In any case, a certainty they will express to everyone is: 'You will only know God by taking the risk of living from him, in a life that is exposed, not protected or withdrawn. And doing this, not just for a time, but for your whole life long. Dare to take this risk over and over again.'

The fear of making a mistake is present when we are young but it can also come back again much later. Some people burst into flame in mid-life, thinking they have discovered the love of their life. They emphasize the errors that surrounded the decision they made when they were young, forgetting that no action on this earth is absolutely pure, otherwise we would be angels.

When the yes to Christ has been confirmed by the person who has known how to listen to you, then go ahead. If you remain in the quagmire of hesitations or regrets, you are wasting time, time that is no longer yours but God's. And the share of error or ambiguity that surrounds every decision will be consumed by the fire of the Spirit of God.

You aspire to live dangerously for the sake of Christ. Each day you will ask yourself the meaning of his word, 'Whoever wants to save their life will lose it'. And one day you will understand what this absolute means.

How will you come to understand? Search. Seek and you will find.

1979, THE WONDER OF A LOVE

# The Radicalism
# Of The Gospel

*Christmas Eve in a women's prison in Santiago, Chile. Mid-
night Mass, then a meal with some of the prisoners. Some have
been sentenced under common law, but others are political
prisoners. Almost all of them are in tears. Some of the faces are
ravaged, others are transfigured with serenity.*

*The priest tells us, 'These are not bad women. Some of them
may be a bit so-so. Some of them are guilty of parricide. But
they are not bad. I know them. I have been coming here every
day for the last twenty years.'*

*As I look into the priest's face and I hear about his daily
faithfulness for so many years, a question wells up inside me
and I ask him, 'Such a passion for God and for communion
with other people, where does all this come from? Did you have
a grandmother or a mother who prayed for you?' 'Yes', he
replied, 'My mother. When I left her in our little village in
Spain twenty-two years ago, she came to the door with me and
said a few words, the last I ever heard her say, "My son,
be a good priest". I never saw her again. She died a year
later.'*

*We had come to visit prisoners, and here we had found a*

*vocation in the very fullest sense of the word, a life in which can be read the absolute of the Gospel.*

No one is built naturally for living the radicalism of the Gospel. In everyone the yes and the no are superimposed.

Yet it is through giving themselves totally that people grow. When they risk their whole life, that becomes a preparation for events beyond their wildest hopes. Far from demolishing them, situations of standstill or discouragement or fierce struggle actually reinforce them. The ways through darkness are travelled stage by stage: the solitude of long nights scarcely lit, with human thirsts unquenched . . . bitterness, that gangrene of the heart . . . the storms . . . all the fears that lurk at life's turning points. . . .

What if the ground has become overgrown with thorns, scrub and briars? Christ lights a fire with the thorns. Do roots of bitterness remain, is loving still impossible? Weakness becomes a crucible where the yes is made and remade and made new again day after day. All that is most threatening in us is transformed into a lever for lifting up our heaviness.

The moment comes when we receive what we no longer even expected. The unhoped for happens. A reflection of Christ within us. Others see its radiance although we are unaware of it. Nothing is to be gained by knowing what light we reflect. There are so many people in the world who reflect the brightness of God without knowing it and perhaps even without daring to believe it.

For those who risk their whole lives, there are no dead ends.

We think we have abandoned Christ, but he does not abandon us.

We think that we had forgotten him, yet he was there.

And we set out once more, we begin all over again, he is present.

That is the unexpected; that is what we did not dare hope for.

Confronted with the radicalism of the Gospel and the risks it implies, many people take fright. Doubt continues within them. Some do not know if they are still believers or not. More than a century ago, when Christians were asking such questions about doubt and faith for the first time, Dostoyevsky wrote from his Siberian prison, 'Until now, and even, I am sure, until the grave, I am a child of disbelief and doubt. How great are the sufferings I have had to endure, and still endure, from this thirst to believe which grows ever stronger in my soul as arguments to the contrary increase.'

Yet Dostoyevsky goes on to insist that in his eyes, 'There is nothing more beautiful, more profound, more congenial, more reasonable, more virile, more perfect than Christ, and not only is there nothing, but with a jealous love I say that there can be nothing. Still more, if someone were to demonstrate to me that Christ is outside of the truth, and that the truth really lies outside of Christ, I would rather stay with Christ than with the truth.'

When Dostoyevsky suggests that the non-believer co-exists in him with the believer, the no with the yes, his passionate love for Christ still remains undiminished. A child of doubt and disbelief, he nonetheless starts out again each day on the journey from doubt towards believing.

1976, A LIFE WE NEVER DARED HOPE FOR

# Fragile As Vessels
# Of Clay

THERE IS one thing we shall never fully understand. Why has God chosen us, fragile vessels of clay, to communicate a part of the mystery of Christ? And why do some people respond to this call and others not at all?

'It is in vessels of clay that we carry this treasure, the Risen Lord', writes a witness to Christ nearly two thousand years ago, 'to make it quite clear that the radiance comes from God and not from us. We are hard pressed on all sides, but not crushed; we are brought down, but not destroyed. Always and everywhere we carry about in our bodies the agony of Jesus, so that in our bodies the life of Jesus may also be revealed' (2 Corinthians 4.7–10).

Revealing and communicating Christ! Being reflections of the Risen Lord through the lives we lead! And yet we know him so little. If we had only our own weak faith or our personal qualities to count on, where would the radiance of God be? It is not for nothing that God has chosen to reveal himself through our human fragility. How easy then it is for us to make our own one of the prayers of the Christians of the early Church, 'You do not look on our sins, but only on the faith of your Church'.

People who consent to communicate a part of the mystery of Christ through the lives they lead, people who place their trust in him even in the arid stretches in their existence, know that their choice can lead them closer and closer to unseen martyrdom. But for them, no matter what happens, no failure is ever final: hard pressed on every side, they are not crushed; brought down, they are not destroyed.

All those who live out the consequences of Christ's call to the utmost see their hearts becoming more and more universal. Refusing to spare themselves, they become capable of listening to everything in others, of sharing their pain and their distress. Far from becoming hardened, far from becoming used to suffering, as the years go by, the openness of their heart becomes boundless.

When everything seems to conspire to make them give up, when they carry within themselves the agony of Jesus that is the suffering of people all over the world, how is it that they are not overwhelmed and exhausted? Here is their secret: at every moment, they hand over everything to Christ, other people's troubles, their own trials, everything that assails them. If they didn't pray for their enemies as well, part of themselves would remain in darkness.

In this continual handing over to God, everything is thrown into him, even our tired bodies. And everything comes to life again to the point that the Risen Christ reveals himself even in our bodies. With our body we sing to him. Everything in us starts to sing again until we are filled to overflowing, '*Jubilate Deo, jubilate Deo*'.

1979, THE WONDER OF A LOVE

# The Unique Gifts In Everyone

*Receiving so many young people in Taizé means being above all people who listen, never spiritual masters. People who want to set themselves up as masters can easily fall into spiritual pretentiousness and that is death for the soul.*

*Indeed, it means refusing to monopolize anyone at all for ourselves. The Virgin Mary shows us a gesture of offering; she did not keep her Son for herself, she offered him to the world.*

*Often we know little of the context in which the lives of the people who confide in us is taking place. That is not the important thing. In any case, answering them with advice or with categorical 'you must's would lead them astray. The essential is to listen to them in order to clear the ground and to prepare the ways of Christ within them.*

*After listening to some of the young people in the church today, I was walking down to the house with one of the brothers. We were saying to one another, 'By the time the young people leave here, if only they have discovered the gift that is placed within them . . . and if in turn they have the burning desire to make the ways of Christ straight for others . . .'.*

Like each and every one of us, Jesus needed to hear a human voice saying, 'You know that I love you'. Three times over he repeated to Peter, 'Do you love me?' Assured of Peter's love, Jesus entrusts him with the Church, 'Feed my sheep'.

To love Christ is immediately to receive from him a greater or lesser part of a pastoral gift. God entrusts one or two people to each person.

This pastoral gift, however small it may be, is a source from which to draw the inspirations for communicating Christ. It makes it possible for Christ to accomplish his pilgrimage in the whole human family.

Even children, without being aware of it, communicate an image of the living God.

Exercising this pastoral gift means above all listening. Listening to what hurts people about themselves. It means trying to understand what is 'underneath' the other person's heart, until they can perceive the hope of God, or at least human hope, even in soil that has been harrowed by tribulation.

And it often happens that people who listen to others are being led to the essential themselves, without the other person even suspecting it.

Growing old. Exercising intuition through a whole lifetime of listening. And finally understanding almost without words those who come to confide.

Listening can bring a mystical vision of the human being, this being who is inhabited by both fragility and radiance, by void and by fullness.

We have all received something of a pastoral heart. And there are unique gifts in everyone. Why do we doubt our own gifts so much? When we compare ourselves with other people, why do we desire their gifts and reach the point of burying our own?

Today's technological age makes our sense of success and failure more acute. A taste for getting on in the world and comparing ourselves with others are inculcated right from childhood. People who do not succeed according to society's standards feel condemned and are disappointed not to have somebody else's gifts.

Comparisons sterilize. When we wish to possess somebody else's abilities, we end up incapable of discovering the gifts in ourselves. When we discredit ourselves, along come sadness and discouragement.

How can we lose our self-esteem when the Spirit of life is pouring out gifts into every one of us? The loss of self-esteem suffocates human beings. It shackles their vital forces and goes as far as making any kind of creativity impossible.

Reacting against this by overestimating ourselves, going after prestige, for example, is no way out. Overestimating ourselves because of social pressure or the judgements of people around us, forcing our gifts artificially, is like forcing a plant in a hothouse.

There is a way in the Gospel in which we meet the gaze of Christ. That way has a name; it is called consenting. Consenting to our own limitations, of intelligence, of faith, of abilities. Consenting too to our own gifts. This is how we really become creators.

1982, AND YOUR DESERTS SHALL FLOWER

# A Yes That Remains Yes

ONCE AGAIN a man of forty-five is speaking in terms that have become commonplace. 'When I married, I was so conditioned that I was unable to stand back and see things clearly. Now, I have found the woman of my life.' Of course, at twenty-three he was not totally clear-sighted. But at what age will he be?

It is impossible to make a choice without renouncing other options for ever. Otherwise, we become erratic, ready to say yes, but only for the moment, with no continuity.

The 'yes' of marriage, like the 'yes' of celibacy for the Gospel, sets us on a knife edge because it involves the entire person, the body and all the inner resources of intelligence, sensitivity, affectivity and imagination.

Giving up any idea of looking back, people who pronounce such a yes say and say again to Christ, all through their lives, 'I trust you, I take you at your word'. If we wait until we are completely lucid before pronouncing a yes that remains yes, are we not in danger of finding ourselves with nothing but leftovers to offer? Once the yes has been pronounced, it becomes the pivot around which a whole life of creativity is worked out, it is a central column around which human beings spin in freedom, a wellspring to dance beside.

Perhaps moments will come when faithfulness is no longer lived out with a spontaneous heart. The yes is a burden, it is accepted without love. Then, the law can take over as our instructor, just for a time, until love springs forth once more.

1973, STRUGGLE AND CONTEMPLATION

# The Sound Of Joy And Gladness

*I have been having some poignant conversations in the church with a young priest. He is questioning himself as to whether he saw clearly enough on the day he made his commitment for life.*

*I have been trying to reflect with him. Who can ever have all the discernment necessary for making a decision? As the years go by, clarity can come in stages, as it were. What was unclear or incomplete to begin with, or even partly mistaken, gradually ripens into the maturity that is necessary for going on and persevering right to our last breath.*

*Inner unity means that we need to assume responsibility throughout our lives for the major decisions we have made. If the abandoning of a life commitment can create a feeling of release at first, if a change of surroundings brings relief, the full consequences can only be measured in the long term. The momentary calm gives way to new questioning.*

*The young priest was saying too that he is afraid of the lack of full humanity in celibacy. But if, in order to become fully human, we had to undergo every experience open to human beings, who would qualify?*

*In chastity, only the desire to see Christ is capable of quenching human thirsts. This is the promise of the Beatitude, 'Happy the pure in heart'. What is confused, sometimes unavowed, is transfigured by fixing our eyes, no longer on ourselves, but on the Living One, the Risen Christ.*

*Did I make myself clear? What will become of him?*

The present crisis of confidence in humanity is stripping away the identity of many of those who have said yes to the priesthood. Some of them are at a loss and no longer know what use they are. Where does the essence of their vocation lie? I can see three specific areas:

Priests are people who set out to find their first and basic love in Christ. They risk their lives, they even give them up for the people who have been entrusted to them.

As those who unbind on earth that which will be straight away unbound before Christ, priests are people who set others free. They practise listening, sounding out the depths of the human person. The older they grow, the more they learn to understand and to give people back their freedom.

And it is the priest who makes it possible for the people of God to live from the paschal mystery in the Eucharist.

How could those who respond to this vocation live it out in isolation, without the rest of us? What can we do for them, and with them? More than we might imagine. By not leaving them to their solitude. By bringing them our trust. By seeking through their ministry of liberation hearts that are poor, reconciled, unified by Jesus Christ. And in so doing give them back 'the sound of joy and gladness'.

Some people say that there are bad pastors. When that is so, let us keep silent. . . . We who struggle within ourselves because we are fragile and vulnerable, how could we demand of them that they be superhuman?

1973, STRUGGLE AND CONTEMPLATION

# The Yes Of A Trusting Heart

IF A TRUSTING heart were at the beginning of everything . . . that is what makes us ready to dare to say a yes for life.

In the Gospel, Jesus talks about a young man who is called to go and work in a vineyard. The young man answers, 'No, I will not go'. But later on, he pulls himself together and goes. That is the yes.

Another person hears the same call and answers, 'I will go', but does not. His yes is a flash in the pan.

This Gospel story is about pronouncing a yes that is very serious, a yes to following Christ for an entire lifetime.

For some people, daring to say yes means responding to Christ's call to the faithfulness of marriage.

In this present time, when so many families break up, will those who choose marriage accept the challenge of persevering right to their very last breath? This kind of faithfulness is a reflection of the faithfulness of Christ himself.

So many children have been scarred through being abandoned by those they love, to the point of losing the sense of trust that is essential for living. The childhood or adolescent innocence of so many young people has been wounded in broken families. Since they have not been able to trust in those who had given them life, their trust in God has waned. Their hearts are like deserts.

Nothing tears us apart as much as the severing of bonds of affection. Disillusionment follows, and the sceptical questioning: what's the use of living? Without love, does life still have any meaning?

Will every home become 'a little church of God', a place of welcome, prayer, faithfulness, and compassion for everyone round about?

There are also those whom Christ calls to follow him by a yes for life in celibacy.

Those who start to understand that this yes commits their entire lifetime can start feeling afraid. They are aware of an immense unknown. A whole lifetime lies ahead: how will I ever hold firm? Who was ever inwardly made for giving themselves in this way? First of all comes hesitation and a no, in a startled reaction that is almost instinctive.

But then one day comes the surprise of finding ourselves already on the way, following Christ. A yes had been placed by the Spirit of God in the core of our being, in what is called the unconscious.

By letting this yes rise up from the depths of ourselves, it is possible to say 'I will'.

The most captivating part of the Gospel story is the fact that the young man began by saying no.

And yet he understood that his refusal was like something alien inside him. If he said no, he was no longer being consistent with the Spirit of God who was alive within him and who, at the core of his being, was saying yes, with the same yes that was in Mary.

Can a vocation that is not desired impose itself to such a degree that one day it has to be accepted? The prophet Jeremiah writes of his experience, 'I said to myself: I will think of God no more; no longer will I speak his name. But it was as if a raging fire was burning deep within me. I struggled to contain it, but I could not.'

A yes because of Christ makes us vulnerable. It makes it impossible to run away from ourselves and from essential solidarity with others.

This yes can be disturbing. It is never easy to be shaken up. The human condition has its fragilities that do not like shocks.

The yes keeps us awake. It keeps our eyes wide open. Could the yes of a vocation drift off or even slumber? Could it try to run away from Christ in the communion of his Body, the Church, so shaken on every side? Could it try to run away from a world that is ridden with suffering?

This yes for life is fire. It is a challenge. Let it burn, this fire that never goes out. And the yes blazes up within. The yes makes us vulnerable. It cannot be otherwise.

1985, A HEART THAT TRUSTS

# THE MYSTERY
# OF COMMUNION
# CALLED THE
# CHURCH

# The Christ Of Communion

WHEN THE brothers and I meet young people, in countries very different to one another, we realize that many of them are seeking Christ, but they are taking him in isolation. Christ in the communion of his Body is being abandoned. The sense of the mystery of the Church is vanishing.

If Christ in the communion of his Body the Church were not being abandoned in this way, then we would not be investing so much of our energies in gathering young people together and in searching with them, not only in Taizé, but throughout Western and Eastern Europe and on other continents as well.

Week after week, as we welcome these young men and women who have come here from all over the world to pray and to seek the wellsprings of faith, we are more and more eager to see each of them discover Christ, not in isolation, but the 'Christ of communion', Christ present in fullness in the mystery of communion which is the Church.

At the heart of this mystery, so many of the young can take the risk of living lives that are vulnerable, of committing themselves for an entire lifetime, and they can become creators of trust and reconciliation, not just among themselves, but with people of all ages, from the very old to little children.

If the Church were nothing but a society, albeit a spiritual one, everything in it would be subject to organization. But then how could it still be this miracle of the Body of Christ, made present and visible on the earth today and always?

Why are we so concerned about the mystery of communion called the Church? Simply because there can be no continuity of Christ in human history if Christians are not part of a people.

Why are we so passionately concerned about the catholicity of the Church, about this universality extended to all its dimensions: the dimension of depth which is the search for a face-to-face encounter in contemplation; the dimension of breadth which is solidarity with the entire human family; the dimension of height which is creativity in simple beauty, in common prayer?

The Church interests us, not for itself, but certainly when it stimulates us to search for God at the wellsprings of adoration, when it prompts us to live Christ for others, and when it becomes a place of communion for the whole of humanity: not a place reserved for privileged people, for the élites of faith, but a place that is open to all of us, the poor of this earth.

Today the Church is faced with one of the great challenges of its history. Is it sufficiently aware that it remains the only place capable of being a leaven of universal communion and friendship in the whole human family?

For this leaven to reach all of humanity, there is one thing that has to come first: reconciliation between Christians without any more delay. If they are not reconciled, how can Christians take a God of love as their reference and how can they awaken other people to God by their own lives? How can we talk about ecumenism if we do not achieve reconciliation, concretely and without delay? If we love only those who love us and who resemble us, are not unbelievers capable of doing as much? The inconsistency that the divisions between Christians represent takes away their credibility and turns the younger generations away from the Church.

1979, THE WONDER OF A LOVE

# Reconciliation
# Within Ourselves

IN THESE years when contemporary society is moving from one crisis to another at an ever more rapid pace, Christians are being shaken too. They are experiencing the subtle sickness of disintegration.

At a time when the ever growing number of people with no knowledge of God staggers the mind, the weight of Christian disunity is a heavy burden to bear.

When Christians are imprisoned in parallel confessions, with their rivalries and their competition, the best in each of them is neutralized.

One saying of Jesus that is becoming relevant as never before is, 'When you bring your offering to the altar and some-one has something against you, leave everything and go and be reconciled first of all'.

'Go first of all.' Not, 'Put it off till later'.

Does not the noble ecumenical vocation need to be trans-figured by the miracle of a reconciliation that is not put off till later?

We are beyond the pioneering stage now. To heal the old wounds and the new ones, it is urgent for the ecumenical vocation to reach a new turning point. It has managed to create remarkable organisations for dialogue, as well as many commissions and research groups. To reach a new turning point, it is essential for all its inner resources, all its structures, all its spiritual insights to be transfigured into the ability to bring about reconciliation here and now.

To give up holding on to our parallel ways, not to look back, to forgive each other, that is the heart of the matter.

Twenty-five years ago, on the eve of the Second Vatican Council, was born the splendid hope of a speedy reconciliation between the non-Catholic Churches and the Church of Rome. In the years that followed, the spirit of unity fostered new understanding and friendship. Remarkable theological documents have been drawn up.

But as time has gone by, the truth has proved to be that reconciliation of the non-Catholic Churches and the Church of Rome seems to have been relegated as it were to a more or less distant future.

Those who longed for this reconciliation are perhaps more numerous than is generally supposed. And there are many people who pursue painstaking theological research and dialogues of all kinds at the instigation of ecumenical institutions. Nevertheless, there still remains the weight of history that has created a kind of unconscious intransigence.

In the face of major impossibilities, what is the good of having hope-filled illusions or of fostering them among the people of God?

God never condemns anyone to standing still. He never closes off the ways ahead. He is always opening up new ones, even if they are sometimes narrow. So the question arises: how can we find a way out of a dead end? Where can we find a road to immediate reconciliation, even if it is an exceedingly small way, for a period of transition?

This way exists. It is not an easy way out. It does not consist in watering down the faith, since it always presupposes the same faith, the same thinking, and the same hope.

This little way forward can only be a personal one. It is an inner way. It is the way of reconciliation within ourself, in our own being.

Without humiliating anyone, without becoming a symbol of abjuration for anyone, it is possible to welcome within ourself the attentiveness to the word of God, so deeply loved by the ecclesial families born of the Reformation, together with the treasures of spirituality of the Orthodox Churches, and all the charisma of communion of the Catholic Church, disposing ourselves day after day to put our trust in the Mystery of Faith.

In the course of long centuries, from the beginnings of the Church, from Mary and the apostles, the motherhood of the Church was one. That motherhood remains one. When, at a give moment, divisions occur, it does not disappear.

*One day, there was a leading Protestant who was passing through Taizé. We had only a few moments together. To help him understand the meaning of our vocation as quickly as possible, I told him the story of my grandmother. His reaction was immediate; this story shed light on our whole search. Why hadn't I dared to speak about it sooner?*

*My mother's mother was a woman of courage. During the First World War, her three sons were fighting on the front. She was a widow and lived in the north of France. During the bombardment, she refused to leave her home so as to be able to give shelter to people who were fleeing, old people, children, pregnant women. She left only at the last minute, when everybody had to flee. Then she went to the Dordogne.*

*Her profound desire was that no one should ever again go through what she had experienced. Divided Christians were killing one another in Europe; let them at least, of all people, be reconciled with one another, so as to attempt to avoid another war.*

*She came from old Protestant stock. In the house where my mother was born, guests were still shown the secret room where they used to hide the pastor in times of persecution. To bring about an immediate reconciliation within herself, she frequented* a Catholic Church. It was as if she knew intuitively that, in the Catholic Church, the Eucharist was a source of unanimity of the faith.

The miracle of her life was that in reconciling within herself the stream of faith of her background with the Catholic faith, she did not become a symbol of abjuration for her own family.

She arrived at my parents' home a year or so later. Worn out with tiredness, she fainted as she came into the house. They carried her away in a red blanket. I can see the scene as if it had just happened.

All this made a great impact on me, and something irreversible took place. Those two gestures of hers, welcoming the most distressed and achieving reconciliation within herself, came to have a lifelong effect on me.

My grandmother's intuition must have given me a Catholic soul right from childhood. In Taizé, I have the impression that I have been continuing along the road that was opened up by that old woman. In her footsteps, I have found my own identity in reconciling in the depths of myself the stream of faith of my background with the faith of the Catholic Church.

Those who are mothers or grandmothers can rejoice. Their faithfulness sometimes leaves traces whose full consequences they will not see in their own lifetimes.

1982, AND YOUR DESERTS SHALL FLOWER

# Wellsprings Of Faith

WHEN TWO people who are separated try to be reconciled, it is essential for each of them to discover first of all the specific gifts that have been placed in the other. If each of them claims to have all the gifts, and wants to bring everything and receive nothing, then there will never be any reconciliation.

The same thing is true for the separated Churches. Reconciliation does not mean that some are victorious and others are humiliated. It implies discovering the gifts placed in the others.

Will, then, the communities born of the Reformation become attentive to that source of unanimity in the Catholic Church that is the Eucharist? Through thick and thin, the Catholic Church has made it possible for the Eucharist to remain a wellspring of unanimity of faith, like an underground river flowing through its entire history, even in the darkest periods (whereas it has always been in the nature of Protestantism to allow each person the possibility of interpreting the words of Christ for himself or herself, including those concerning the Eucharist).

Adorable presence of Christ in the bread and the wine, the Eucharist cannot be received mechanically, out of habit, but always in a spirit of poverty and repentance of heart, with the soul of a child, right to the evening of our life. At the beginning of this century, when Pope Pius X opened the Eucharist even to children, he showed a rare intuition.

The Eucharist is there for those who are hungry for Christ. When one of the baptized is hungry for the Eucharist and wishes to approach it, when Christ calls, who would dare to refuse?

By remaining before the Eucharist during long inner silences when nothing seems to be happening, many people have matured the great decisions of an entire lifetime. They have allowed themselves to be penetrated down to the very depths of their being.

'My Kingdom is within you.' Even when the heart senses nothing, the Eucharist is constantly bringing these words of Christ to life, even for someone who hardly dares imagine it.

While the Catholic Church is above all the Church of the Eucharist, it has another special gift. It has known how to set men apart to bring forgiveness, to unbind on earth what is immediately unbound in the Kingdom, to lift from our shoulders the burden that is too heavy to bear, to wipe away even the most recent past.

Confession gives us the opportunity of expressing as spontaneously as possible what weighs on our conscience. No one is able to say all that there is to say about their faults. But if we say what springs to mind at the moment, that in itself is immeasurable for receiving the unimaginable forgiveness of God in the sacrament of reconciliation.

At the present time, some people feel that it is necessary to play down or even to deny sin, so as to eliminate feelings of guilt. It has become clear, however, that such an attitude, far from removing guilt, diffuses it throughout the whole person, spreading it out to such an extent that it cannot be reached, far less uprooted.

Some people, with great seriousness, make frequent use of confession, since they find it so necessary to live from this visible sign that wipes out all the past. Others, just as serious, make less frequent use of it, since they are so sure that God holds them in his forgiveness.

In both cases, confession is the essential place for rediscovering the freshness of the Gospel, for entering a new birth. It is there that we learn to blow away our feelings of remorse, like a child blowing away a dead leaf. There is the happiness of God, the dawning of perfect joy.

As for the Protestant Churches, their specific gift has been above all to be the Churches of the Word. The Catholic Church too has always found in Scripture a wellspring for living from God, but the best in Protestantism has been the discovery of the impact of the Word of God in personal life.

This Word from God must be situated in Scripture as a whole, not taken in isolation; it must be put into practice immediately.

When we remember the quality of some of the great Protestant divines of the seventeenth and eighteenth centuries, those whose writings and poems were turned into chorales and hymns of an intensity rarely achieved, by Johann Sebastian Bach, for example, then we can better understand to what extent the Word of God was loved and taken seriously in people's lives, how much it stimulated a whole inner life, how much it penetrated, stirred and worked through Protestant Christians down to their very depths.

As for the finest of the gifts of the Orthodox Churches, this means entrusting oneself to the Spirit of the Risen Lord. He shines through the liturgy to such an extent that certain non-believers come to sense his presence. So often in their history, it is there that Orthodox Christians have drawn the courage for going, through faithfulness, to the extreme of loving.

Can the course of ecumenism be set free if no appeal is made to a pastoral ministry on a worldwide scale? A man named John made me move forward in that perspective. By his ministry, John XXIII opened my eyes to this vocation of universality.

During the last conversation I had with John XXIII, shortly before his death, I grasped that his prophetic ministry had perhaps been misunderstood and that, as a result, a turning point of ecumenism had been missed. He had declared publicly,

'We will not put history on trial. We will not ask who was right and who was wrong.' He had taken huge risks. Going against the advice of many people, he had not hesitated to invite non-Catholics to the Second Vatican Council. He asked forgiveness for the past and he was ready to go a long way. I understood his sorrow at receiving no reply.

If each local community needs a pastor to stimulate communion between those who always tend to scatter, how can there be a hope of visible communion between all the Christians of the world without a universal pastor? Not at the top of a pyramid, not at the head (Christ is the head of the Church), but at the heart.

As universal pastor, the Bishop of Rome is today being called to be free to profess prophetic intuitions, free to exercise an ecumenical ministry which fosters communion between all Christians, even those who refuse his ministry for the moment or have been refusing it for a very long time. What can we ask of this pastor other than that he make the wellsprings of faith more explicit for each new generation?

Is it not the responsibility of the 'servant of the servants of God', not only for Catholics but for non-Catholics too, in a word, to confirm his brothers and sisters, so that they may be of one faith and of one mind? 'Peter, confirm your brothers.'

Perhaps I have hurt somebody by writing in this way, or hung a stone about someone's neck. When it is too heavy for them, let them hang it about my own neck. Not that I am pretending to be able to bear it, but I shall try.

1979, THE WONDER OF A LOVE

# A Parable Of Communion

FACED WITH the urgent need for the Gospel to be made present at the heart of the human family, we are conscious of how limited are the resources of our community when compared with the vast horizons that are opening up on this eve of a new millennium.

Who are you, little community? An efficient instrument?

No. Never. Fine as that may be.

Perhaps a group of men who have come together to be, humanly speaking, stronger, with an eye to realizing their own aim?

Not that either.

So, could we be living a common life in order to be comfortable together?

No. The community would then become an end in itself, and that would open up the possibility of making cosy little nests in it. Being happy together? Certainly, but in the context of the offering of our lives.

Who are you, little community, spread out in different parts of the world?

A parable of communion, a simple reflection of that unique

communion which is the Body of Christ, his Church, and through this, being also leaven in the human family.

What is your calling?

In our common life, it is possible to move forward only through discovering ever anew the miracle of love, in daily forgiveness, in heartfelt trust, in a peace-filled way of seeing those who are entrusted to us. . . . When we move away from the miracle of love, all is lost, everything vanishes.

Little community, what might well be God's desire for you?

To be made alive by drawing nearer to the holiness of Christ.

Whether in Taizé or in the fraternities, each brother takes part in the one parable of communion. More through perseverance of character than through action, more by what he is than by what he accomplishes. In this way, the small acts of faithfulness of each day prepare and sustain the great continuities of a whole lifetime.

As we go our way, we are always being led to take risks. Our vocation makes us vulnerable. And yet I have never had any doubts about the continuity of our community. It will endure. There will be trials, no doubt, but it will come through them.

Does not seeking reconciliation between Christians with unshakable resolve mean becoming like a living rock around which waves of enthusiasm or scepticism come breaking?

Avoiding the ecumenical vocation of reconciliation between Christians so as to situate ourselves solely at the nerve centres of the contemporary world can have a certain attraction for us. Among non-believers, there is sometimes so much clear thinking, generosity, and lively appreciation of all that is human. In their company, we have chanced to breathe more freely than in certain Christian circles that are so closed in on themselves.

Whoever is following Christ, whoever is bold enough to say yes, is choosing love. Even when the incomprehensible happens, such a person consents not to hold back. Stepping back would perhaps mean suffering less. But in every case that means protecting ourselves and letting other people make themselves vulnerable.

Why does a relationship with Christ in isolation, without the communion of his Body, the Church, lead believers to turn in on themselves and become individualistic, either on their own or with a few other people?

Through his own life, Christ allows us to perceive an answer to that question. It bears the name of holiness. He came for everyone, not just for a privileged few.

Anyone who draws near to the holiness of Christ in the mystery of communion which is his Body, the Church, is brought irresistibly, like one of the poor of God, to seek complete openness, the outlook of a child, a universal heart. Such a person becomes a leaven of reconciliation, and there can be no hope today of a vast awakening of Christians without reconciliation.

1985, A HEART THAT TRUSTS

# Reawakened From Within

HOW OFTEN the same question comes up in daily conversations with the young people from different countries! 'Why do you love the Church? Its structures hurt us so much.'

Should people who sometimes suffer from the Church run away from it? But doesn't running away from the Body of Christ lead straight to abandoning the Risen Christ by the roadside? Just as human beings can only be changed from within, and never by reprimands that come from outside, isn't remaining within, with infinite courage, the way to transform rigid structures? Harshness and pressures have always been doors that lead to blackmail, and that is an attack on human freedom.

It was a first-century Christian who grasped the fact that communion in the Body of Christ is a fundamental reality that finally carries everything else along with it. 'The reality is the Body of Christ', writes Paul to the Colossians, 'and let no one try to deprive you of it.'

In recent years, as contemporary society becomes more and more anonymous, great numbers of little groups of Christians have sprung up. They are a kind of antidote to a secularized world. With a freshness of the Gospel, these groups bridge the gap between faith and life. Forms of commitment that are adapted to a rapidly changing world are being discovered in them.

Because of the provisional nature of their life, an inevitable feature of these little communities is their extreme fragility. In order to survive, some of them turn into exclusive little circles whose options cut them off on every side. There are people who let themselves be cast in any mould, however esoteric its form, provided they feel good together in a small number. When Christians are fragmented into such tiny particles, what happens to communion in the Body of Christ?

Moreover, the large communities which are called 'parishes' do not exactly engender enthusiasm. On our travels across the continents, we cannot help but notice that the great majority of Christians normally meet for prayer in these large local communities. But the young in particular are ill at ease in them when their aspirations are not recognized and they find no scope for their energies. Some of them are bored in the churches, and boredom is a spiritual suffering.

Could we not be in a period of birth and maturing in common prayer? If the abundance of words in our churches is a source of weariness, soon we shall start giving priority to singing in our prayer.

If young people could join in the Eucharist, at least every Sunday, and then prolong it by staying on in church and singing, they would already be creating a space of adoration.

From the depths of the night of humanity a secret aspiration is welling up. Caught up in the anonymous rhythm of planning and schedules, contemporary women and men have an implicit thirst for the one reality that is essential: an inner life, and signs that point to the invisible.

When common prayer gives a foretaste of the joy of heaven on earth, people come running from everywhere to discover what they had been unconsciously lacking.

Nothing contributes more to communion with the living God than a common prayer that is both meditative and accessible to old and young alike. The high point of this prayer is the singing which never ends and which continues afterwards in the silence of the heart when we are alone again. Winds may blow, bringing dryness in their wake and enlarging the deserts . . . the unquenched thirsts find peace.

When the mystery of God is made accessible by the simple beauty of symbols, when it is not smothered under an excess of words, then an all-embracing common prayer opens the way to the joy of God in our human world.

And the presence of all the generations, from the very old to little children, is a powerful symbol. It helps us realize that there is only one single humanity.

1982, AND YOUR DESERTS SHALL FLOWER

# A Childhood Of The Church

*We spent Christmas Eve in the home for the dying run by Mother Teresa's Sisters in Addis Ababa. They put down some mattresses at the back of the room for the sick children. Some of the littlest ones couldn't get to sleep. One was always wanting to switch on the light, another one to get up, and so it went on. When we wakened in the morning, we could see in their eyes how happy they were to find us there. Did they think we were the Three Wise Men?*

*I am still preoccupied with something I saw in Bangladesh more than a year ago. In a narrow alleyway, a child was crouching on the ground, carrying a baby on one arm, and trying to lift a second baby with the other arm. When he managed to get hold of them both at once, he slumped to the ground. An impression of the wounded innocence of childhood. Why is it impossible to take care of such children? More than a year later, my heart has still not got over it.*

*Children! They are such a joy and such a mystery in our lives! Who can ever express sufficiently all that they are able to communicate, through gifts unknown to themselves that have been placed in them by the Holy Spirit? They make us understand*

*something of the living God by the trust they show us, by a word*
*they say or a question they ask, so unexpected that they*
*awaken us to a life in God.*

Speaking about the realities of the Kingdom of God, Christ says
that only those who receive them with the heart of a child can
understand them.

God makes himself accessible to hearts that are simple and
who immerse themselves in his trust. When adults or old people
have a childlike soul, they are able to be mindful of a childhood
of the Church.

A childhood of the Church at the present time: not being
nostalgic for the early Church, but kindling in the Church of
today the spirit of childhood. First and foremost that means
simplicity. It is also heartfelt trust and wonder. Through it, slick
manoeuvring and compromise fade away. All administrative
relationships are transfigured into approaches of communion.
The spirit of childhood never manipulates and never uses anyone for its own ends. And the Church, even when crushed by
trials, does not allow itself to be imprisoned in sadness and
resignation.

Not resignation, but trust. Not inertia, but a kind of inner
letting go: abandoning ourself to the living Christ, to his Holy
Spirit.

Trust of heart can be undermined through misunderstandings; it blossoms in unceasing rebirths.

If childhood does not have a monopoly of trust, it does
contain a measure of innocence that marks us for life when it
has been wounded. Everything is registered, just like on a piece
of soft wax.

For God, human beings are sacred, consecrated by the
wounded innocence of childhood. Is it not from there that
people draw the energies for creating and for loving? And is it
not the same for the mystery of communion which is the
Church?

Sometimes we adults think that a pessimistic attitude is proof
of seriousness. We leave no room for wonder. So how can we

still be in tune with the realities of the Gospel?

The spirit of childhood is a crystal-clear way of looking, and far from being simplistic, it is lucid as well. The various aspects of a situation, positive and negative, are no strangers to it. It has nothing childish about it. It is imbued with maturity. It implies infinite courage.

The spirit of childhood does not let itself be held up by the hardened structures of the Church. It looks for ways of getting through them, as the stream water finds its way through the frozen earth in early spring.

1982, AND YOUR DESERTS SHALL FLOWER

# If Festivity Were
# To Vanish

IF FESTIVITY were to vanish from people's lives . . .

If we were to wake up one fine morning in a society that was well organized, functional and contented, but devoid of any spontaneity . . .

If Christian prayer became an intellectual discourse, secularized to the point of losing all sense of mystery and poetry, leaving no room for the spirit of praise, for intuition, for affection . . .

If the overburdened conscience of Christians made them say no to a happiness offered by the One who, on the Mount of the Beatitudes, proclaims 'happy' seven times over . . .

If the peoples of the northern hemisphere, worn out by activity, were to lose the wellsprings where they can find the spirit of festivity: festivity that is still so alive in the hearts of the peoples of the southern hemisphere . . .

If festivity were to disappear from the mystery of communion which is the Church, would there still be a place of communion in the world for the whole of humanity?

And always the same for each generation, the thirst for communion is intense among many of the young:

Communion with humanity in its struggles and aspirations, in these years where we are witnessing a crisis of confidence in humanity.

Communion with Christ. For so many of the young, simply remaining in the presence of God is vital, whether or not they can achieve a dialogue when they do so.

If the spirit of festivity in us were to disappear, would we still have the strength to seek ever anew for communion with the new generations?

1971, FESTIVAL WITHOUT END

# A LEAVEN OF
# TRUST IN THE
# HUMAN FAMILY

# The Dawn Of An Entirely New Future

CHRISTIANS TODAY are living at a time when the vocation to universality, to catholicity, confided to them by the Gospel can find unprecedented fulfilment.

Since the fourth century, few periods in history have been more decisive for Christians.

Are they going to have hearts that are big enough, imaginations that are open enough, love that is afire enough to respond to one of the primary calls of the Gospel? Will they take the risk of being reconciled each new day and, in this way, be a leaven of trust between nations and races in the dough of the human family which, in order to survive, is aspiring to unity throughout the world?

As the twentieth century draws to an end, there are people who are caught up in a spiral of fear. Their creative powers are chilled by fright and they are allowing themselves to be sucked under.

It is true that the questions that must be asked in order to achieve peace on earth are so vast and complex that they leave us breathless.

Far from being thrown off balance, many Christians and non-believers too, are keenly aware that midnight is upon us and the dawn of an entirely new future is on its way.

From this, they are acquiring a sense of urgency. Preparing themselves for this turning point in history, they are making this new civilization their own, and they are a leaven of trust in the world.

Fear in the face of spectacular scientific and technical developments? No. Science and technology are able either to build or to destroy. It all depends on the use to which they are put.

Science and technology are so beneficial when they allow us to sense the unlimited possibilities generated by human ability. Methods of food production unknown till now are going to provide solutions in regions where endemic hunger reigns. Are we not beginning to produce protein from algae, and soon even with the aid of bacteria, and to double their quantity in twenty-four hours? Great discoveries are alleviating or curing physical and moral suffering. A universal civilization, based on the new communications media, on information systems, and on satellites, is creating a world in which boundaries are being overcome.

On the other hand, it is equally true that scientific techniques are capable of destruction. Incredible means of war are able to annihilate part of the human race. This plunges the peoples of the earth into an ocean of fear. They are terrified by the vision of an apocalyptic future born of violence, injustice and threats of destruction.

Yet the entire human family wants peace, never war. Minute is the number of 'hawks' who want war, infinite are those who are ready to be ferments of trust among all the peoples of the earth. It was in 1963 that a man with tremendous spiritual authority, John XXIII, called for a 'world government'. That intuition of world peace is a seed that has been planted in the earth.

Christians are people who are neither optimistic nor pessimistic. They know that history is not merely a chain of mechanical causes and effects in which everything is relentlessly determined in advance. History gives intuitive forces their place too.

Without rejecting the deterministic laws that are fundamental to their research, there are scientists today, agnostic or otherwise, who are discerning limits and discontinuities and an element of the unforeseeable. The century of determinism is showing itself to be humble in the attitude of its most able researchers. It may be that this will lead to a twenty-first century of profound faith.

So many creative powers are lying dormant in every human being, nourished by the passion of an inner life. Far from submitting passively to the harshest events, it becomes possible to build even with them. It is not only events that make us happy, but even some of the most unbearable situations, and even the failures, which can become factors that drive us forward. The creative powers are somehow reawakened by these events, with a view to transfiguring the world.

*I have been invited several times to Poland to take part in the Silesian miners' pilgrimage at Piekary. Some of them go by foot for four hours and then stand several hours more during the prayer. The crowd is so enormous that you cannot take it all in at one glance, even from the top of the hill. I have been asked to talk to them about Mary:*

*'Not one of you Polish workers thinks you have an influence on the development of the human race. I want to tell you that the contrary is true. It is not those who appear to be in the front ranks who bring about changes in the world.*

*'Look at the Virgin Mary. Neither did she think that her life was essential for the future of the human family. Like the Mother of God, you are the humble people of this world who are preparing the ways that lead to a future for everybody. Your faithful waiting on God is carrying forward many other people throughout the world.'*

Ways forward filled with hope are opening up at the present time. It is important to remember that very often, in the most difficult periods of history, a small number or women and men throughout the world have been able to turn the course of historical development, because they hoped against all hope. What had been doomed to disintegration entered instead into a stream of new dynamism.

1985, A HEART THAT TRUSTS

# Meeting Those Who Cannot Believe

IN TAIZÉ, year by year, our vocation has made us more and more open to other people. It has awakened in us an interest in those who were farthest away from us. Without a passion for the mystery of communion that is the Church, we would never have discovered this friendship with so many people throughout the world.

Concern for dialogue has made us attentive to everything that is human. Who would not burn with desire to understand another human being in the struggle of their existence: to recognize in their eyes the flame that has gone out or, on the contrary, the serenity they have won over themselves; to regard the restrained attitude of the other's whole personality, or the scars of their conflicting impulses; the generous gift of the self or the firm resolve to hold on to it.

The spirit of mercy disposes the heart of stone to be changed into a heart of flesh. It leads us to a strong love that is devoid of sentimentality, that caricature of sensitiveness. It refuses to dramatize in a subjective way. It invites us to welcome our neighbours and events, whoever and whatever they may be, in peaceful trust.

How does it come about that certain non-believers, who claim not to know God, are people full of mercy? They open up ways of peace, they are men and women of communion, they show so much attention to peacemaking among everyone.

It is possible to believe that, although they do not profess an explicit faith, these people are bearers of Christ unawares. Could not this be the outcome of the prayers of so many Christians down through the ages? Human beings are hearing God without knowing him, they are being obedient to him, they are living lives of charity. How can we avoid applying the words of Christ to them, 'They are going before us into the Kingdom'? They are opening doors for us, they are paving the way.

Numerous are those who are children of light without knowing it. It is easy to recognize them. They are full of concern for their neighbour and they flee the works of darkness, all that is unclear and lacking in transparency.

The dialogue with people who do not believe allows us to discover in them what they do not recognize in themselves, the mystery of a hidden presence.

It goes without saying that it is only people who find their own support at every moment in the Word of God and in the Eucharist who can speak in this way. Otherwise, the result would be relativism. To say that there are people who are following God unawares could constitute an invitation to cease all combat for Christ. What then would be the good of praying, or of remaining in God's presence?

1965, THE DYNAMIC OF THE PROVISIONAL

# Taking Risks For World Peace

IN THIS AGE, when awareness of human rights has never been so strong, the law of 'might is right' is still rife in many parts of the world. Humanity is experiencing violence, rumours of war and armed conflicts.

In the Gospel, peace bears the important name of reconciliation. This name requires commitment and takes us very far. Being reconciled means beginning a whole new relationship; it is a springtime of our being. What is true between individuals goes for nations too. What a springtime a reconciliation of the nations would be, especially between East and West.

A whole young humanity in both hemispheres is eagerly waiting for the frontiers which are separating the peoples to be brought down, and they are not afraid of taking risks for world peace. These young people have certain basic characteristics:

In their search for peace, they refuse to support vested interests, whether they be those of a continent, a nation, a race or a generation.

They are aware that first among all the conditions necessary for world peace is a more just distribution of the goods of the earth among everyone. The unequal distribution of wealth is a wound dealt to the whole human community.

Among those seeking for greater justice, there exist two different aspirations. They are complementary. Some are more inclined to use all their energies to bring immediate help to the victims of injustice. Others are concerned first and foremost with acting on the causes and the structures which foster injustice.

Youth who are seeking for peace also know that it is only when equal trust is shown to all of the peoples of the earth, and not just to a few of them, that what is tearing them apart can be healed. So it is essential never to humiliate the members of a nation whose leaders have committed acts that are inhuman. Essential also is infinite attention towards so many men and women who today are living on foreign soil as exiles or immigrants. If every home were open to someone of another background, the racial problem would be partly solved.

In order to share material goods better between North and South, and to repair what is broken between East and West, sincerity of heart is necessary. Who could appeal for peace, be they political leaders or not, without achieving it within themselves? 'Be sincere of heart and be steadfast', wrote Ben Sira, twenty-two centuries ago.

In the critical situations of our time, many men and women are prepared to go on ahead of trust among the peoples of the earth, through the lives that they are leading. They are seeking in God the energies to persevere. They are committing all of their inner and spiritual resources to anticipating peace and reconciliation, not on the surface but in depth. They are well aware that it is not with weapons of power that they are being called to struggle, but with hearts that are pacified. They refuse to take up positions that are partisan.

Peace begins inside ourselves. But how can we love those who are oppressing the weak and the poor? Harder still, how can we love our opponent when he professes faith in Christ? God gives us the gift of praying even for those who hate. God is wounded with the innocent.

'Love your enemies, do good to those who hate you, pray for those who treat you badly.' Grasping the meaning of these words needs maturity and also the experience of having come through inner deserts of our own.

In the ocean that lies deep within the human being, there resides a longing. Day and night, it receives the answer: peace.

1982, AND YOUR DESERTS SHALL FLOWER

# The Sign Of Christ's Forgiveness

*Soweto, Johannesburg. Even more than in the lack of material things, poverty here consists in the segregation that forces one million blacks to live in this neighbourhood.*

*A meeting with a young black who is just out of prison. 'The whites are afraid of us', he says. 'They are trying to force us to accept their scale of values, but these values are materialistic and individualistic. They go counter to our own. We blacks want to express the brotherhood of everybody. In this way, according to our tradition, people who are the same age as ourselves are our brothers and sisters, the younger ones are our little brothers and sisters, and the older people are our mothers and fathers.*

*'In the last few years, the spirit of fear and mistrust has grown and it has led to a situation where war and violence have become institutionalized. The situation often produces acts of violence and court cases. There is fear and bitterness. In the end, some people are leaving the country.*

*'Faced with this situation, we have discovered the necessity of moral force and forgiveness. The whites have learned so little about forgiving. It is there that we discover the grace of God in our lives.'*

An unexpected visit to the Cape. I had learned only on the previous day that we were expected there. In a black neighbourhood where we thought we would only be meeting a few friends, a whole crowd had gathered for prayer. They were singing. The human voice communicates the cry from the depths like no other form of expression.

We were welcomed on to a platform, and a microphone was passed to me. I made allusion to the man of God from Africa my parents had met one day when I was five years old. He blessed me. From then on, my mother often used to say that faith was disappearing in Europe, but the Gospel in all its freshness would come back to us from Africa. I assured these people that the blessing of long ago was finding fulfilment at that very moment.

Next, it was someone else's turn to speak. Yet I was saying to myself that my words had been so inadequate. I asked the two brothers who were with me if I should take the microphone once again and they said yes. Then I tried to express through a gesture all that was in my heart. I explained to these Africans, 'I would like to ask your forgiveness, not in the name of the whites, I could not do that, but because you are suffering for the Gospel and you are going before us into the Kingdom of God. I would like to pass from one of you to another so that each of you can make the sign of the cross on my palm, the sign of the forgiveness of Christ.'

The gesture was understood immediately. Everyone made it, even the children. It seemed to last an eternity. Spontaneously they burst into songs of resurrection.

1982, And Your Deserts Shall Flower

111

# Simplifying And Sharing

THE BREATH of God is sweeping through the world to such an extent at the present time that signs of quite a different civilization are appearing at the heart of one that exalts material goods and power.

One of these signs is an unprecedented awakening of the Christian conscience with regard to sharing. In the past, Christians seemed not to concern themselves with the issues of justice, human rights and the just distribution of material goods. Now, they are attentive to people forgotten by society and more and more of them are at work to find solutions.

Sharing, far from being merely 'relief work', is the giving of ourselves.

In heartfelt trust, one of the pure joys of the Gospel is to simplify ourselves within, and this leads to an ever simpler life style and to sharing: sharing with God in prayer and sharing with human beings on this earth.

Simplifying and sharing never mean a life of severe austerity, filled with judgements on other people. Simplifying invites us to arrange everything in the simple beauty of creation.

Without artistic creation, there is a kind of puritanism that can predominate, bringing guilt in its wake. Art itself comes from God.

There are artists' hands which allow us to discover faces from the Gospel, of Christ, of the Virgin Mary, to such an extent that simply by looking, we can sense the mystery of God. And in music, it can happen that the inexpressible leads us to prayer and the veil is lifted on the inconceivableness of God.

Poverty is a word that scorches the lips. When I was writing the Rule of Taizé in 1952, I hardly dared use it. My pen could scarcely bring itself to write it. Believing that the spirit of poverty lay first of all in simple sharing, I preferred to speak of a commitment to community of goods 'without fearing possible poverty'.

If we have to give up many material possessions, the spirit of poverty goes still farther. Poverty of means could lead us to look for compensations elsewhere, for example, by commandeering other people and forcing them to enter into our scheme of things.

The spirit of poverty embraces the whole of our being. The external signs of poverty are not enough. They do not necessarily prevent us holding on to a human ambition, a need for power, or a desire to dominate our neighbour that is sometimes disguised by appearances.

Sometimes, a puritanical attitude can prevail. This consists in acting poor and, in other words, looking drab, while all the time wealth is concealed behind the faded exterior. 'Happy the heart that is poor.' If the spirit of poverty becomes synonymous with sadness, how can it correspond to the first Beatitude? The spirit of poverty is to be found in the joy of the believer who trusts in God. It manifests itself in outward signs of joy.

The spirit of poverty does not lead to complacency. One Beatitude cannot be exaggerated at the expense of the others. The poor are gentle; they remain the poor of Christ. Without charity, poverty is nothing; it is a shadow without light.

1965, THE DYNAMIC OF THE PROVISIONAL

# The Deepest Wound Of Our Time

*I have been spending a few days with my brothers in New York.
The district they live in, right in the centre of Manhattan, is
called 'Hell's Kitchen'. Being there made my heart overflow.*

*The brothers are living on the top floor of a building that has
been more or less patched up. Once, the ceiling gave way and
left everything open to the sky and the rain. The people here are
living by their wits. They have no regular jobs. The neighbourhood is dangerous at night. Sometimes you can hear shrieks,
even in the building itself. On our street one morning, the trash
collectors were seen removing arms and legs from one of the
bins. The apartment is burgled periodically.*

Anyone who is aspiring to live the 'Sermon on the Mount'
wants to become a companion of the poor.

But where are the poor? Everywhere on this earth.

In many places in the world, like Calcutta, there are homes
for the dying which are visible. . . . In the West, there are many
young people who find themselves in homes for the dying which
are invisible. Outwardly, they look like all the others; they are
studying, they are learning a trade, or they are working, but they

do not know where to sink their roots.

So many of the young today are a prey to subtle doubt, even those who are thirsting after a spiritual life. The schemes for changing society worked out by previous generations leave them bewildered. Some of them have been marked for life because of being abandoned by those they love or they have been wounded to the core because their families have broken up. They no longer see the point of their existence and they wonder if life still has any meaning. They too are the poor of the earth.

Talking about the parable of the prodigal son, a young man from New York said, 'In my family, it was not the son who went away, it was the father who left us'.

There are some parents who certainly provide for their children's material needs, yet in fact they are away from home as far as the children themselves are concerned.

In the West, the hearts of many of the young, and of the less young, are dying away of rejection.

Indeed, being abandoned by others is the worst trauma and the deepest wound of our time.

Generation gaps. Worlds turned upside down. There are elderly people in the West who want for nothing materially, but who are ending their lives in isolation, as if there was nothing left for them but to wait for death.

There are so many elderly women and men who think they are worthless and who feel they have done nothing with their lives. Yet they know how to listen to other people without being judgemental and to understand everything about them.

They know how to love. They know how to suffer. They are filled with a trust that is transparent. Who will kiss their worn hands to thank them for preparing ways forward for other people?

1985, A HEART THAT TRUSTS

115

# Living The Unhoped For

HIDDEN WITHIN every human being, there is a Life that rouses our hope. It opens up ahead of us a way of transformation, both for ourselves and for everybody.

Will you focus your attention on it?

Without this hope anchored in your heart of hearts, and without this transformation that lies beyond your own personality, you lose all inclination to forge ahead.

This is not a sheer projection of your own desires, it is a hope that incites you to live the unhoped for, even in situations that appear to be dead ends.

In your relation with Christ, you will find the courage to go on waiting for developments of history to break wide open, even those that appear to be the most inescapable.

This hope engenders a momentum of creativity and it overturns the inevitability of injustice, of hatred and of oppression.

In the relation with the Other, hope comes from him. It is this hope that remakes the world.

When you set up the centre of your universe in yourself, you are plunged into self-absorption and all your powers of creation and of loving are out of joint.

To shift the centre, and for love to be kindled there, you are being offered the same fire as every human being in the world: His Spirit within you.

His stimulus, his spontaneity and his inspiration have only to awaken and right away life becomes strong and intense.

Rooted in the mystery of communion that is the Church, will you be a bearer of living waters? Will you quench the thirst of all those who are seeking for the wellsprings of life?

We are not servants of peace and trust just by wanting them. We still have to go to the wellsprings and reconcile struggle and contemplation within ourselves.

Who could willingly accept being a mere conformist in prayer, in justice or in peace? Who could stand other people saying about them, 'They talk but they do not act. They say "Lord, Lord", but they do not do his will. They say "Justice, Justice", but they do not practise it. They say "Peace, Peace", but within them there is war'?

Many other people are obsessed with this as well as you. They are fervently seeking Christ in contemplation and they are paying for peace and trust in the human family with their lives.

Do not let yourself be caught in the alternative between commitment to the poor and the quest for the wellsprings of life.

Not struggle *or* contemplation, but *both* of them together, the one springing from the other.

The radicalism of the Gospel is much too demanding for you to pass judgement on those who do not understand.

And even when you are not understood, do not come to a halt. It is yours to risk your life in this way.

A hand to grasp yours? To lead you on the way? No one can do that for anyone else. . . .

No one, but he who has already recognized you. . . .

1976, A LIFE WE NEVER DARED HOPE FOR

# A Short History
# Of Taizé

### THE BEGINNINGS
In 1940, Brother Roger was twenty-five and the Second World
War was raging in Europe. For several years, filled with a
passion for the absolute, he had been thinking of setting up a
monastic community dedicated to reconciliation. So he left
Switzerland, where he was born, which was too peaceful for his
taste, and moved to France, where his mother came from, to be
close to the war and to the suffering which it entailed. He wrote
later on, 'The more a believer wants to live something absolute
for God, the more is it essential for that absolute to be rooted in
situations where people are suffering'.

As he looked for a house to live in, he arrived in the little
Burgundy village of Taizé, where he was met by an old
woman. He explained his plans to her and she said, 'Stay here,
we are so isolated here'. For him it was like the voice of God
speaking to him through the words of a poor old woman.

Taizé was two kilometres from the demarcation line which
was at that time cutting France in two, and in the house he
acquired he hid political refugees, many of them Jews, who
were fleeing from the German occupation zone. He lived in

Taizé from 1940 to 1942. On his own, he was praying three times a day, as the community he was thinking of would do in the future. After the house had been searched several times by the Gestapo, he finally had to leave Taizé and could not return until the end of 1944.

## THE COMMUNITY, A PARABLE OF COMMUNION

When he did return to Taizé in 1944, Brother Roger was accompanied by the first three brothers, whom he had met during his absence from Taizé. In 1949, seven of them undertook monastic commitments for life: celibacy, accepting the ministry of the prior, and community of material and spiritual goods. Brother Roger was the prior. In 1952, he wrote 'The Rule of Taizé'.

The first generation of brothers are of Protestant background, yet the roots of the community go right back before the Reformation as it takes its place within the monastic family. Taizé is ten kilometres from Cluny, which in the Middle Ages was one of the most famous centres of monastic life in Europe, and it is also not far from Cîteaux, another landmark in monastic history. Later on, Brother Roger gave symbolic significance to the geographical location of the community. 'Taizé is like a shoot grafted on to the tree of the monastic life. No doubt there is a meaning in the fact that we are placed between Cluny and Cîteaux. On the one side, there is Cluny, with its humanity, its sense of moderation and continuity. Cluny, which held such an attraction for so many Christians seeking unity within themselves and with other people. On the other side, Cîteaux, renewed by St Bernard, with his acute sense of urgency and his reforming zeal and refusal of all compromise of the absolute nature of the Gospel. In their footsteps, he would like to blend the sense of urgency and the sense of long continuity.'

Gradually, the community has grown through the years. The first Catholic brothers were able to enter in 1969. Today the community is made up of 90 brothers, Catholics and from various Protestant backgrounds, from over twenty different countries. By its very existence, the community is a sign of

119

reconciliation between divided Christians and between separated peoples and it constitutes what Brother Roger calls 'a parable of communion'.

If reconciliation is at the heart of Taizé's vocation, that is never seen as an end in itself but rather that Christians be like leaven: leaven of reconciliation among human beings, of trust between the peoples, and of peace on earth.

The community does not accept gifts or presents for itself. The brothers do not even accept their own family inheritances. They earn their living and share with others entirely through their own work.

When the brothers were about twelve in number, in the 1950s, some of them set off to live at certain of the nerve centres of the world, to be witnesses of peace there and to be alongside people who are suffering from poverty. Today, in small fraternities, there are brothers living in poor neighbourhoods of New York, in North-East Brazil, in Kenya, Korea and Bangladesh. They are sharing the same conditions as the people around them and they are there to listen to them and to support those who are trying to find solutions to the difficulties there.

Brother Roger himself spends periods of time in places that are experiencing particular difficulties, to be close to those who are undergoing trial and sometimes to draw attention to certain specific situations. He has made several visits to the neighbourhood where the brothers are living in New York. He spent some time in Chile following the *coup d'état*, and thereafter, each year has seen him among the poor in Calcutta or in South Africa, in the earthquake region of southern Italy or in Lebanon, in Haiti or drought-stricken Mauritania, in a slum in Madras or in Ethiopia. Every year, he visits Eastern Europe where the community has many friendships with the young and the less young which go back over twenty-five years.

## WELCOMING YOUNG PEOPLE AND THE INTERCONTINENTAL MEETINGS

Taizé has been welcoming young people in steadily increasing numbers ever since 1957–58. From Sweden to Portugal, from

Scotland to Hungary, and from far beyond, they come to take part in meetings which last one week and which are centred on the search for the wellsprings of faith.

Since 1987, the numbers coming from the countries of Asia, Africa and South America have shot up. Mexico, India, Haiti, South Africa, Japan, Chile . . .; through the year, over a hundred countries are represented in the meetings. At the same time, the presence on the hill of people from Eastern Europe has become more and more tangible, especially people from Poland, Hungary and Yugoslavia. Many families with children come to spend a week in Taizé together with young families from other countries. Without counting the thousands of pilgrims who pass through Taizé every day and spend just a few hours, the intercontinental meetings bring together every week between 3,000 and 4,000 young people in summer, and between 500 and 1,000 in spring and autumn. Easter, Pentecost and All Saints are high points in the year.

Responsibility for the travel expenses of the young people who come from far beyond Europe is assumed by parishes within Europe itself. After a period of preparation in Taizé, the young visitors spend several weeks in the parishes who have invited them. For centuries, it was above all from Europe that the Gospel was transmitted. Today, these young people, coming from countries where the Gospel is sometimes more alive, are able to take part in a new evangelization of Europe and in a springtime of the Church.

Through the years, hundreds of thousands of young people, looking for the meaning of their lives, have passed through Taizé and their visits there have been marked by the central theme of bringing together faith and commitment, and interior life and human solidarity. Several generations of youth have acquired there, not only a sense of prayer and a more universal vision of the Church, but also an attention to human rights, an international awareness, a trust in foreign peoples and a sensitiveness to peace and to the sharing of cultures.

Three times a day, the common prayer takes place in the 'Church of Reconciliation' which was built in 1962 and which is frequently enlarged by adding on several marquees. The 'Taizé chants' have become characteristic of the worship. These are made up of a simple phrase that is taken up again and again at some length, in various languages, and they express an essential reality that is quickly grasped by the understanding, and little by little is interiorized by the whole personality. In the evening, after prayer, brothers stay in church to listen to those who want to talk individually about some difficulty or some question which is preoccupying them.

Every Saturday evening, the prayer is like an Easter vigil, a feast of light. A beautiful symbol brought back from Russia by Brother Roger is 'the prayer around the cross' every Friday evening. The icon of the cross is laid on the ground, and people place their foreheads on it for a moment, thus laying down their own burdens as well as those of others, and in this way accompanying the Risen Christ who is in agony for all those who are suffering trials.

Since 1966, Sisters of Saint Andrew, an international Catholic community founded 750 years ago, have been living in the neighbouring village and are responsible for part of the work of welcoming visitors.

When Pope John Paul II visited Taizé in 1986, he introduced himself as a pilgrim and said, 'One passes through Taizé as one passes close to a spring of water. . . . I want to express to you my confidence with the words with which John XXIII, who loved you so much, greeted Brother Roger one day, "Ah, Taizé, that little springtime".'

## A PILGRIMAGE OF TRUST ON EARTH

In 1970, Brother Roger launched the idea of a 'Worldwide Council of Youth' whose main gathering was held in 1974. During years when the young were experiencing discouragement and were moving away from the Church, the Council of Youth brought hope and inspired them to take part in the reconciliation of Christians and in the fostering of peace in the world. To give time for it to mature and to await the moment when it would be taken up once again, the Council of Youth was provisionally scaled down to a minimum in 1979, gradually taking on the form of a pilgrimage of reconciliation.

In fact, it was in 1982 that in Beirut, Lebanon, Brother Roger invited the young and the not-so-young to set out on a 'Pilgrimage of Trust on Earth'. The pilgrimage does not organize people into a movement centred on Taizé but encourages them to become pilgrims of peace and bearers of reconciliation in the Church and of trust on earth, through their involvements in their own cities and neighbourhoods, in their parishes and villages, and to do this with people of every generation, from little children to the very old.

Once a year, Brother Roger writes an open letter whose aim is to support the pilgrimage. These letters are written in places where he is living for a time, often situations of great poverty: the 'Letter from Calcutta', 'from Warsaw', 'from Haiti', 'from the Desert', 'from Madras', 'from Ethiopia', 'from Russia'. Each letter is translated into between 25 and 30 languages and serves as a basis for discussion and meditation throughout the following year.

Like the stations of a pilgrimage or the halts on a journey, from time to time Taizé animates large gatherings in major cities like Montreal, New York, Washington, Madrid, Dublin, Lisbon or Brussels. The participants, who come from far and wide, are welcomed by the parishes of the city and the prayer is held in the cathedrals. Sometimes there are meetings in Eastern Europe, as in Warsaw, Dresden and East Berlin. At the end of every year, there is a European Meeting, attended by 20,000 to 30,000 people, held in London, Paris, Rome, Cologne, Barcelona or Wrocław (Poland). Occasionally, there are Asian meetings, like those held in 1985 and 1988 in Madras, or East–West meetings, such as Ljubljana, in Yugoslavia, and Pécs, in Hungary. In 1988, on the occasion of the celebrations of 1,000 years of Christianity in Russia, through an appeal, Taizé had one million Russian New Testaments printed and sent off to Christians there.

In his preoccupation with respect for human life, Brother Roger has sometimes been able to intervene discreetly in tense situations in various parts of the world. In the name of the young, he also undertakes public approaches in favour of peace. Underlining the symbolic character of these approaches and clearly showing that they are not undertaken for himself, as an older man, but for those whose future is at risk, he is accompanied on these occasions by children from several continents. He has had meetings with the ambassadors of the Soviet Union and the United States in Madrid as well as with leaders of several nations. He has handed over to Javier Pérez de Cuéllar, Secretary General of the United Nations, suggestions from the young on how the UN can create trust among the peoples. Mr Pérez de Cuéllar writes, 'The Pilgrimage of Trust which Taizé is animating with the young is contributing to bringing us nearer the ideal of peace to which we are all aspiring'.

In all of these ways, Taizé is seeking expressive gestures and symbols which, beyond the present difficulties, evoke the coming of a springtime of the Church, a Church which, at the heart of humanity, is a 'land of reconciliation, of sharing and of simplicity'.

---

**Address: 71250 Taizé Community, France.**

---

# To Learn More About Taizé

**OTHER BOOKS BY BROTHER ROGER**
*And Your Deserts Shall Flower*
Australia, New Zealand and UK: Mowbray
*A Heart That Trusts*
Australia, New Zealand and UK: Mowbray
*Awakened from Within: Meditations on the Christian Life*
USA: Doubleday & Company, Inc., 666 Fifth Avenue, New York, NY 10103
*Living Springs* (forthcoming)
Containing 'The Rule of Taizé'

**WITH MOTHER TERESA OF CALCUTTA**
*Meditations on the Way of the Cross*
Australia, New Zealand and UK: Mowbray
India: Asian Trading Corporation, 150 Brigade Road, Bangalore 560 025
USA: The Pilgrim Press, 132 West 31 Street, New York, NY 10001
*Mary, Mother of Reconciliations*
Australia: St Paul Publications, 60–70 Broughton Road, Homebush, NSW 2140

India: Daughters of St Paul, 143 Waterfield Road, Bombay 400 050
Philippines: Claretian Publications, UP, PO Box 4, Quezon City 1101
UK: Mowbray (address below)
USA: Paulist Press, 997 Macarthur Boulevard, Mahwah, NJ 07430

*The Letter from Taizé*
Published every two months in ten languages, giving news from across the world, suggesting themes for reflection in groups and parishes, containing texts for meditation, prayers, and a Bible reading for each day.
Address: 71250 Taizé Community, France

## BOOKS
*A Pilgrimage of Trust on Earth*: colour booklet with photographs and texts about the community and the meetings in Taizé. (UK: Mowbray)
*Taizé: Trust, Forgiveness, Reconciliation*: colour photographs, texts by Brother Roger and a visitor's impression of a stay in Taizé. Booklet. (UK: Mowbray)
*The Story of Taizé* by José Luis González Balado (3rd revised edition). (UK: Mowbray)
*A Universal Heart: the Life and Vision of Brother Roger of Taizé* by Kathryn Spink. (Canada: Fitzhenry & Whiteside Ltd, Toronto; UK: SPCK; USA: Harper & Row, Publishers, Inc., 10 East 53rd Street, New York, NY 10022)
*The Taizé Experience*: colour photographs by Vladimir Sichov with texts by Brother Roger. (Australia and New Zealand: St Paul Publications; UK: Geoffrey Chapman Mowbray; USA: The Liturgical Press, Collegeville, MN 56321)

## VIDEOS
*Taizé: That Little Springtime*: 26 minute documentary. (UK: Mowbray; USA: Journey Communications, PO Box 131, Mount Vernon, VA 22121)

*Taizé: Trust is at Hand*: 28 minute documentary on the community, meetings in Taizé, Madras, Hungary, Paris, at the UN, etc. (UK: Geoffrey Chapman Mowbray; elsewhere Taizé)

## MUSIC
*Praying Together in Word and Song*: booklet with suggestions for prayer together and a selection of Brother Roger's prayers. (UK: Mowbray; USA: GIA, 7404 S Mason Avenue, Chicago, IL 60638)
*Music from Taizé*: 2 volumes; vocal and instrumental editions. (Australia: Collins Dove, PO Box 316, Blackburn, Vic. 3130; UK: Collins Religious, Westerhill Road, Bishopbriggs, Glasgow G64 2QT; USA: GIA)

## CASSETTES
*Canons et litanies – Cantate – Resurrexit – Alleluia*; also available on CD. (Australia: Rainbow Book Agencies, Northcote, Vic. 3070; UK: Mowbray's Bookshop, 28 Margaret Street, London W1N 7LB; USA: GIA)

Unless otherwise stated, all books and cassettes can be obtained from:
**Australia and New Zealand**: Charles Paine Pty Ltd, 277–279 Sussex Street, Sydney, NSW 2000
**Canada**: Donald E. Meakin, Meakin & Associates, Unit 17, 81 Auriga Drive, Neapen, Ontario K2E 7Y5
**Ireland**: Veritas & Co. Ltd, 7–8 Lower Abbey Street, Dublin 1
**South Africa**: Oxford University Press, PO Box 1141, Cape Town 8000
**United Kingdom**: Mowbray, Stanley House, 3 Fleets Lane, Poole, Dorset BH15 3AJ; religious bookshops.

Brother Roger is the founder and prior of the Taizé Community. From the outset, he has sought to open up ways of overcoming the divisions between Christians and the conflicts in the human family. Today the community is made up of ninety brothers, Catholics and from various Protestant backgrounds, from some twenty different countries. Taizé has become a place of pilgrimage where every year many thousands of young adults from all over Europe, and far beyond, go to pray and to prepare themselves to be promoters of peace, reconciliation and trust throughout the world. In 1988, Brother Roger was awarded the UNESCO Prize for Peace Education.